Advance Praise for
The 5 Simple Truths of Raising Kids

"This book provides an excellent overview of youth development. Educators and parents always look for advice and they will find many ideas about how to understand, support, and educate adolescents."

—**Gil G. Noam** is the Founder and Director of the Program
in Education, Afterschool & Resiliency (PEAR) and
an Associate Professor at Harvard Medical School

"In this wonderful book, Brad stands up for today's kids, debunks all the claims that they're somehow worse than the last generation, and offers sound, research-based advice on how parents and communities can do a better job raising them. Having worked for many years with all kinds of kids—from the privileged and the achieving to the abused and disabled—Brad has an easy familiarity with how kids think. He channels their emotions into his chapters."

—**Neil Howe** is a renowned authority on generations and
social change in America. An acclaimed author and speaker,
he is the nation's leading thinker on today's generations.

"*The 5 Simple Truths of Raising Kids* will immediately change your relationship with your tween or teen—and I promise it will be a change for the better! R. Bradley Snyder gives deep insight and practical guidance for what we all know is the most difficult and ultimately most important phase of parenting. Vulnerable teens seem to push parents and adults away, but they still need us. Snyder's easy to read book tells us how we can shift our perspective to remain a key player in our kids' lives. He answers all the questions parents ask me about teens, including the toughest ones about TV, driving, texting, sex, and drugs. Now I have the answers!

For parents, teachers, community leaders, and any adult who cares about the next generation of our citizens, *The 5 Simple Truths of Raising Kids* is an urgent "must-read!"

—**Carol J. Evans**, President, Working Mother Media, and Author,
This is How We Do It: The Working Mothers' Manifesto

"Every week my inbox is flooded with parenting books to review all with a common theme—our kids are in a desperate state and need immediate intervention. R. Bradley Snyder's book, *The 5 Simple Truths of Raising Kids* takes away the dread and replaces it with hopefulness and humor.

The good news? Our tweens and teens are in pretty good shape (arguably in a better spot than my peers in Generation X). Snyder cuts through the hyperbole of modern statistics and gives parents tangible takeaways.

I'm better prepared for the tween years that I'm facing, having been able to discern fact from sensational headline. This doesn't mean parents have a free ride, but it does mean we're not in a cataclysmic situation. With care and attention, Snyder gives parents the tools they need to guide their kids through these years."

—**Nicole Feliciano**, Editor & Founder of MomTrends.com,
a parenting lifestyle website

"Unlike many parenting books, this one makes you feel better about being a parent: better grounded in your own experience of growing up, better versed in current research on children, better prepared to respond positively and effectively to the worrisome things kids do. Brad's calm and authoritative style effectively defuses the anxiety parents so often feel when faced with hot-button issues like bullying and the siren song of television and social media. He reminds us that the needs of children, and the stages of development through which they pass, have not changed. Whether the context is food or video games, parents and children together can identify the central issue, and apply Brad's five simple truths to figure out what to do."

—**George C. Brackett**, Former Director, Technology in
Education Program, Harvard Graduate School
of Education, and Founder, Codman Academy
Charter Public School, Boston

"I had the opportunity to work with Brad conducting many kid-focused studies at Cartoon Network. I've seen him walk into a room full of kinetic nine-year-olds, and quiet them into rapt attention using only his calm, inquisitive voice. It was chilling, actually. He's like a kid whisperer. Brad's humanity is infectious, and his dedication to his work is inspiring. I can think of no better mentor to parents needing reassurance that kids are good, and everything is going to be okay."

—**Art Roche**, creative executive for digital media
and family entertainment

"R. Bradley Snyder has spent the last 25 years working with, *and for*, young people. The list of organizations that depend upon his understanding of 'tweens and teens' is wide-ranging and impressive, from parole boards to TV networks, communications and marketing gurus, school-boards, and parents among them all.

Now his *The 5 Simple Truths of Raising Kids* offers his understanding and insight to anyone seeking advice on dealing with the generation too often regarded as 'aliens.'

They're not, says Snyder. Rather 'kids are kids,' a statement more significant than the words themselves. Think of the 'problem with teens' you see lamented in the popular press. Nearly every one of those problems—social network addiction, teenage crime, sex drugs and rock and roll, etc., etc.—is overstated, says Snyder. The solution? The simple (if little recognized) act of true parenting.

His reassuring guide to parenting is well-argued and filled with pertinent examples offered in clear, direct prose. You'll learn from his book, and enjoy the lessons. Like Spock two generations ago, Snyder's worth your attention. Well done!"

—**Richard Peck**, Author of *Something for Joey*

"In an age where we're constantly sounding the alarm, it's a pleasure to get sound advice from a guy who's done his homework—and a relief to know, in these days of helicopter parents and tiger moms, that I have a fighting chance as a parent."

—**Amy Silverman**, Managing Editor, Phoenix New Times, author of
award-winning stories about juvenile justice and mental health.
Co-teacher, Mothers Who Write workshop, blogger, girlinapartyhat.com

"*The 5 Simple Truths of Raising Kids* offers insightful lessons about how parents can enjoy their children more, while being better prepared for the challenges of parenting in contemporary society. Snyder uses his experience, research, and clear vision to write a book that all parents should read."

—**Aaron Kupchik**, Ph.D., Author of *Homeroom Security: School
Discipline in an Age of Fear*

"In this book, Brad stands in front as a defender for our kids. They need one. In this day and age where we, as a public, seem to be okay with our children being demonized and blamed for what we consider to be their surprising lack of attention, their lower moral values and somehow irresponsible embrace of technology, Brad cuts through the misinformation and rhetoric to share with us a clear picture of what our kids' essential needs are, who our kids really are, and why they do the things they do. Without being preachy, he reminds us of our responsibility as parents, teachers, and communities and that, guess what, raising kids is hard. We have to pay attention, we have to practice what we preach, we have to be consistent. And at the end of the day, if we do these things, we will have cultivated a next generation who is smart, independent, generous, forward thinking and responsible and really, what's more important than that?"

—**Terry Kalagian**, Independent Producer/Consultant

"Brad Snyder knows kids. And just as importantly, he knows how to articulate his knowledge of how kids think in a way that takes the mystery out of how they think and behave. In my years of working in children's television, Brad's ability to explain in a clear, concise way what motivates today's youth was always the quickest path toward understanding how best to communicate to kids.

One of the recurring themes Brad presents, that 'kids are kids,' effectively demystifies a generation that has grown up with technology and influences my generation and others never had to wrestle with. Knowing that at a base level being a kid hasn't changed in many ways levels the playing field with memories of adults own time as a youth. That Brad goes on to expertly explain how these new technologies and influences factor into how young people today learn and interact with the world around them is like having a Rosetta Stone in many ways: Brad's book helps adults find common ground with young people, then explains how our differences aren't as mysterious or frightening as we once thought. Because, again, kids are kids.

Brad's book gives kids credit for being thoughtful, curious, and social human beings without demonizing their natural motivations and behaviors. And these core beliefs lay a foundation where adults can build effective two-way communication with the young people they hope to understand better.

Brad's frequent illustrative references from popular culture made reading and processing this book a pleasure, and while there is frequent scientific data backing up his learning, I never felt like I was being lectured at. Brad's conversational tone is warm and informative; he's the kind of expert you'd love to talk to over dinner. And as such, I think the lessons he's learned resonate more deeply."

—**Steve Patrick**, Children's Television Producer

"Brad Snyder's fresh perspective makes for a page-turning guide that's both practical and inspiring. I recognized the kids in my life on every page, and found brand new understanding of familiar patterns. Every parent and mentor should read this book."

—**Molly Chase**, Host of the Saturday Morning Submarine Adventure Show at HUGE Theater in Minneapolis, MN

The 5 Simple Truths of Raising Kids

The 5 Simple Truths of Raising Kids

How to Deal with Modern Problems Facing Your Tweens and Teens

R. Bradley Snyder

demosHEALTH

NEW YORK

Visit our website at www.demoshealth.com

ISBN: 978-1-936303-39-7
e-book ISBN: 978-1-617051-29-6

Acquisitions Editor: Noreen Henson
Compositor: diacriTech

Author photo by Art Streiber.

Medical information provided by Demos Health, in the absence of a visit with a health care professional, must be considered as an educational service only. This book is not designed to replace a physician's independent judgment about the appropriateness or risks of a procedure or therapy for a given patient. Our purpose is to provide you with information that will help you make your own health care decisions.

The information and opinions provided here are believed to be accurate and sound, based on the best judgment available to the authors, editors, and publisher, but readers who fail to consult appropriate health authorities assume the risk of injuries. The publisher is not responsible for errors or omissions. The editors and publisher welcome any reader to report to the publisher any discrepancies or inaccuracies noticed.

Library of Congress Cataloging-in-Publication Data

Snyder, Brad (R. Bradley)
  5 simple truths of raising kids: how to deal with modern problems facing your tweens and teens / Brad Snyder.
    p. cm.
  Includes bibliographical references and index.
  ISBN 978-1-936303-39-7 (alk. paper)
  1. Parenting. 2. Child rearing. 3. Parent and teenager. 4. Teenagers. 5. Preteens. I. Title.
II. Title: Five simple truths of raising kids.
  HQ755.8.S6432 2013
  649'.1—dc23

                                                                                    2012021786

Special discounts on bulk quantities of Demos Health books are available to corporations, professional associations, pharmaceutical companies, health care organizations, and other qualifying groups. For details, please contact:

Special Sales Department
Demos Medical Publishing, LLC
11 West 42nd Street, 15th Floor
New York, NY 10036
Phone: 800-532-8663 or 212-683-0072
Fax: 212-941-7842
E-mail: rsantana@demosmedpub.com

Printed in the United States of America by Hamilton Printing.
12 13 14 15 / 5 4 3 2 1

For my parents,
Russell and Mary Ann Snyder

Contents

Foreword

Often the most helpful and insightful pieces of advice seem to be the simplest ones. I found this out while preparing for the birth of my first child. I was nervous about being a parent, as are most first-time parents. I began to read some articles online and leaf through a few of the many books written to help prepare first-time parents, which only made more even more anxious. I learned that there is so much to think about as a parent from day one. Of course, there are the safety basics, such as sterilizing baby equipment, putting the baby down to sleep on her back, and so on. I also learned that how I acted might shape my child's self-esteem, learning readiness, life satisfaction, SAT scores, approach to romantic relationships, and on and on—the list, and anxiety that came from it—were overwhelming. But then I found Dr. Spock's classic book, *Baby and Child Care* (a revised and updated edition). Certainly, Dr. Spock and the pediatricians who have revised the book since his death have packed several very useful facts and pieces of specific advice into the text, but I took from that text one very simple overall lesson: Love your child, be kind, caring and responsible, and follow common sense. Put more simply: Don't worry so much. To me, this was a godsend, as it freed me from thinking about all the ways that I am likely to make parenting mistakes, reduced my anxiety, and let my excitement and joy of impeding parenthood take over. The advice is simple, and for me it was much more helpful than the more complex warnings about all the hazards facing my unborn child.

In this book, Brad Snyder follows a similar path by reminding us that parenting need not be as complicated as many so-called experts and parents seem to make it. Why? Because kids aren't as different from us, or as violent, as mature, or likely to be victimized by strangers, as most people think. Society tends to exaggerate the dangers that kids pose to us and the dangers that they face. The result is that we treat them like criminals at young ages while protecting them from any possible threat in a way that can stifle their growth. We worry so much about kids, both as victims and perpetrators, that we get in the way of their progress.

A good example of this is what we currently do to protect children in public schools. Fears about school crime are high, and in response we have created a slew of policies intended to make schools safer. It is now normal for schools across the United States, especially high schools, to have surveillance cameras, random searches by drug-sniffing dogs, locked gates around the perimeter, zero tolerance, and armed police officers stationed full time at the school. Yet school crime, along with youth crime in general, is much lower now than it was twenty years ago. What's more, there is no good evidence that these law-and-order policies have any effect on school crime, and some evidence that they might actually make schools more dangerous (they can cause youth to resent the school and as a result misbehave in school more often). These policies also increase dropout rates, they cause enrolled students to miss class time unnecessarily, they increase racial and ethnic disparities in educational outcomes, and they're very expensive to implement. In other words, we are so worried about the safety of our children when they are at school—despite the fact that most schools are very safe, and safer than the schools that their parents attended—that we have created all sorts of policies that seem to do kids more harm than good.

We can and should do better, both as parents and as citizens who elect the politicians responsible for policy-making. Therein lays the importance of this book, since Snyder gives us the coaching we need in order to do better. He tells us how and why kids aren't as bad as they sometimes seem, and how they're more like we were at their age than we at first realize. Armed with this knowledge, we are in a better position to care for them. We can let kids be kids, while we do a better job of creating a safe, nurturing environment that allows them to learn from both their mistakes and their successes.

In addition to calming our fears, Snyder also offers a basic, easily digested primer on childhood development. He explains a bit about what makes kids tick: what motivates them, how they think, what influence adults have on kids, and why they roll their eyes at us so much. With this understanding in mind, he then tackles several topics that are particularly worrisome to many parents: texting, video games, social media sites, television, and bullying. Though kids' uses of these technologies can make them seem distant and different from what we were like as kids, not as much has changed as at first appears. In his calming, Dr. Spock—like manner, Snyder eases fears by reminding us that 1) kids are good, and 2) being a loving, caring, responsible adult is still the most important thing we can do to help kids.

This message is even more powerful, more important, because it runs against the grain of the literature on kids. Looking at some of the currently popular books on kids and parenting, we see that as parents we do a whole lot *wrong*. Some of us are helicopter parents, suffocating our kids; others teach our children a sense of entitlement that leaves them ill prepared for the actual trials and hardships of adult life; still others allow our children so much time on social media sites that they tune us out. And then we have the mean girls, overscheduled kids with no time to be kids, and an obesity epidemic to boot. Some of these claims have validity, and others don't. But they all focus on the negatives of our actions as parents and the negative aspects of contemporary kids' behaviors. In the process they raise our level of anxiety rather than calm us down, so that we might be able to see the good in our children and enjoy their qualities while helping them grow and learn.

My advice is to read *The 5 Simple Truths of Raising Kids* with an open mind. You may find that some of your beliefs about kids simply don't hold water when considering the evidence, and you may learn a bit about what parenting approaches are most helpful to kids. But most of all, you may learn to enjoy your kids more. At the very least, I hope you enjoy reading this well-written, insightful book.

Aaron Kupchik, Ph.D.
Associate Professor of Sociology and Criminal Justice
University of Delaware
Author of *Homeroom Security: School Discipline in an Age of Fear*,
and *Judging Juveniles: Prosecuting Adolescents in Adult
and Juvenile Courts*

Acknowledgments

I am grateful for Amy Silverman's encouragement to start this book. I am grateful for Robert Kempe's counsel when early attempts to publish this failed and because he introduced me to Noreen Henson. I am grateful for Noreen Henson's enthusiasm for the project and for all of the support I have received from Demos Health Publishing. I am grateful for all of my clients who have allowed me opportunities to study kids, and especially for Cartoon Network and the Council of Juvenile Correctional Administrators. I am grateful for my colleagues, Yasmine Asfoor and Chad Burggraf, for their professional assistance. I am grateful for the love and humility afforded by my family, especially my father-in-law Richard Peck, my mother-in-law Donna Peck, my sister Cindy Interdonato, and my aunt Barbara Roberts. I am grateful for my amazing wife, friend, confidant, and collaborator, the brilliant and beautiful Laura Peck. Finally, I am grateful for my daughter, Ella Snyder-Peck, about whom none of what I write applies.

The 5 Simple Truths of Raising Kids

1

Introduction to the 5 Simple Truths of Raising Kids

In an episode of *The Simpsons* from the show's fifth season, a self-help guru named Brad Goodman comes to Springfield. During his seminar, he says the following:

> Right now, I want each of you to try something interesting. There's no trick to it. It's just a simple trick! Now, close your eyes for a moment and really listen to that inner voice inside, your inner child. Listen! What's he saying?

In writing a book entitled *The 5 Simple Truths of Raising Kids,* I cannot help but feel like I am saying, "There's no trick to parenting. It's just a simple trick!"

For many years, companies like Cartoon Network and Marvel Comics and nonprofit and government entities like the U.S. Justice Department have hired me to interview, survey and otherwise study kids to find out what they like and what they dislike, what they fear and what they hope for, and generally what they do and why they do it.

As you might imagine, I've learned some things about kids. Some of what I've learned comes from surveying and interviewing over 100,000 children and adolescents, some of what I've learned comes from working in and running direct service programs in Phoenix, Boston and New York City, and some of what I've learned comes from my own observations.

I've always known that this information is valuable to companies that market to or make products for kids. After all, they pay for the findings. Likewise, I have witnessed governments and nonprofits use the information to increase the impact or efficiency of their youth-serving programs. However, more and more parents are coming to me and asking me to speak at their churches, schools and community centers, asking me to help them understand their kids. OK, some ask me to "fix" their kids, but I know what they mean. These parents often have a difficult time believing what I tell them. I think it's because what I've learned about the current generation of young people flies in the face of what glossy magazines and television morning shows would have us believe.

The entirety of my research and professional experience distills down to these 5 simple truths:

- Kids are kids
- Kids are good
- Kids need parents
- Kids need adults
- Kids need communities

Really, the only thing simple about these truths is that they are easy to remember and very few of the words have more than one syllable. One of the truths may seem redundant, at least two of the truths contradict everything that's been on *The Today Show* for the last five years, and one is frustratingly obvious. This is why I did not want to call the book *The 5 Simple Truths of Raising Kids*. I wanted to call the book *The 5 Super Awesome Principles That Will Blow Your Mind, Cause You to Question Everything You Believe About Kids, and Conceivably Change Your Political Views*, but Noreen, my Editor, said that it was too long and came too close to plagiarizing John Cusack's character, Gib, in *The Sure Thing*.

The book is divided into two halves. In the first half, I address each truth individually. I present theory, research and statistics to demonstrate the validity of each truth, and I explain the implications of each truth. Where possible, I use examples from my work and from the research world to illustrate the legitimacy and power of each principle.

Why I Say "Kids"

Much of this book focuses on what the industry calls "tweens." The term was coined to describe young people between childhood and adolescence. The age range typically is set at 8 to 12 years old. Whether or not tweens actually exist is worthy of debate, but the term is useful, particularly because it is used so much in popular media.

This book also discusses "teens," a term typically used to describe 13- to 19-year-olds. When I describe teens, I am employing a slightly stricter definition. I use teens to describe middle school and high school students. When they reach college age, all bets are off as far as I am concerned.

I use "kids" to describe them all, tweens and teens alike. I know the term falls in and out of favor with educators and other professionals. I know that some people may find it pejorative. However, it has face validity. When you hear somebody refer to "that Roberts kid," for example, you know they are not talking about a preschooler or a young child. In your mind's eye you picture somebody the age of Bart Simpson or Joanie, Ritchie Cunningham's "kid sister" from the television series *Happy Days*. In other words, you picture a 10- to 13-year-old an individual towards the middle of the tween-to-teen continuum. Besides, tweens and teens refer to each other as "kids."

The first half of the book is by far the denser of the two. There are many numbers and charts, and several experts are mentioned by name. I apologize for this. If you want, you can take me at my word that the 5 simple truths are valid and skip to the second half of the book, but experience tells me that you might need more convincing.

The second half of the book uses the 5 simple truths to address kids' behaviors as they relate to five fairly contemporary phenomena:

- Television
- Videogames
- Social networks

• Texting

• Bullying

These chapters address popular perceptions about each phenomenon. I explore how kids are behaving in each of these domains and, using the 5 simple truths, I offer explanations for their behaviors. In each chapter, I also use the 5 simple truths to create strategies for promoting the types of successful behaviors that you, as an adult who cares about kids, want for those kids in your life.

There is one other thing you should know. Throughout the book I talk about adults and kids that I have met who have impacted how I think about these issues. They are all real. For adults, I use their real names. For kids, I change their names and alter certain details to hide their identities.

Later in *The Simpsons* episode that I mentioned, Lisa complains about the message of self-help guru Brad Goodman. She says, "This is madness. He's just peddling a bunch of easy answers." If, after reading this book, you still believe that my tricks are nothing more than simple tricks, I hope you will reply as Carl did to Lisa. Is this a bunch of easy answers? "And how!"

2

Kids Are Kids

"Do you know what I want more than anything?" The question was posed to me by a 10-year-old boy named Martin. Martin was a kid who could most conveniently be described as "at risk." His mother and he were poor. They lived in a small, clean apartment that the mother struggled to maintain while working the best job she could find with only a high school education.

I had been mentoring Martin for a number of months as part of a volunteer program.

"Do you know what I want more than anything?" he asked. Without waiting for my response, Martin answered his own question, "a backyard."

Martin did not want a videogame or a high-definition television or a smartphone. He was not interested in texting or social networking or his online profile. Martin wanted to build a fort and climb a tree. He wanted to play.

Martin's wish did not surprise me. Over the last several decades in my professional capacity, I have asked countless 10-year-old boys from all walks of life what they like to do when they are not in school. They tell me that they play sports, organize games with other kids in their neighborhood, and pursue hobbies.

Of course, many boys tell me that they like to play videogames, watch television or go online, but these are not by any measure the most frequently offered responses.

The fact is that despite a preponderance of technology, omni-present media, and new catchphrases to define them, kids are kids. The best research on the topic and my own experience indicate that in many significant ways the current generation of young people is not that different from previous generations. In fact, there is no credible evidence to support that who tweens and teens are on the inside—who they are developmentally—has changed at all over the years.

To think that kids today are not kids, or that they are fundamentally different than we were at their age, is to place an artificial barrier between us, as adults, and the kids in our lives, a barrier that thwarts positive communication and growth.

WHO TWEENS AND TEENS ARE DEVELOPMENTALLY

Barely a week goes by without me having what I call the "Kids These Days" discussion. It typically happens at receptions or on airplanes after a new acquaintance learns that I study children and adolescents. The discussion is characterized by statements of bewilderment—like, "those darn teenagers"—and comparisons—like, "in my day, we didn't have . . . " and "when I was a kid, we would never think to . . . "—and denying that our parents expressed the exact same bewilderment and dismay about us when we were kids.

It is a discussion I have had all too often with too many people, including parents, educators and childcare professionals, and it goes something like this:

ADULT: Brad, what is up with young people today?

ME: What do you mean?

ADULT: Well, you've seen them, how they dress. And they are so disrespectful. And that music they listen to, you cannot make out the words. And they are always listening to it. You cannot even ask them a question.

ME: Didn't our parents say that about us?

ADULT: This is different. We never acted this way!

ME: And didn't our parents' parents say that about them?

ADULT: This is different.

ME: How?

ADULT: It just is.

It isn't different. Kids are kids, and they are driven by the same impetuses that motivated us when we were their age. In fact, understanding these rather timeless motivations that all humans share can help connect us with the kids in our lives and even explain kids' behaviors in their modern world.

It is useful to think of developmental psychology as a journey in which one's thoughts are determined by one's capacities, which in turn are related to one's wants and needs. A journey is an appropriate metaphor because kids are not all at the same developmental stage. Tweens and teens, the focus of this book, are at very different stages of the journey.

The Tween-to-Teen Developmental Continuum

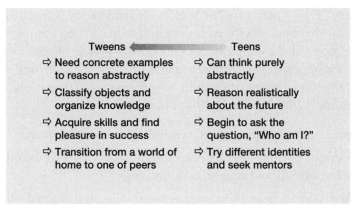

Tweens ⬅ Teens

⇨ Need concrete examples to reason abstractly

⇨ Classify objects and organize knowledge

⇨ Acquire skills and find pleasure in success

⇨ Transition from a world of home to one of peers

⇨ Can think purely abstractly

⇨ Reason realistically about the future

⇨ Begin to ask the question, "Who am I?"

⇨ Try different identities and seek mentors

Kids at the younger end of the tween-to-teen developmental continuum, towards the beginning of the journey, need concrete objects to reason abstractly. It's a big difference between them and kids towards the end of the journey. A developmentally older teen has the ability to reason abstractly. A younger tween does not have that ability.

The example I use is one of a griffin. A developmentally young tween might be able to imagine one if she has seen a lion and an eagle, but she would not be able to if she did not have concrete examples like these to draw upon. A teen can reason abstractly without concrete examples, and this is a big difference between kids at the beginning of the tween to teen developmental continuum and kids towards the end.

Likewise, as kids journey across the tween-to-teen developmental continuum they transition from a world of the home, where their primary caregivers, their parents, are the only entities that matter, to a world where the opinions and preferences of their friends and peers become much more important, giving rise to peer pressure, clichés and social networking.

Another significant difference is that kids at the younger end of this tween-to-teen developmental continuum feel compelled to do different things than kids at the older end. Younger tweens feel compelled to classify objects and organize knowledge, they feel compelled to develop skills, and they feel compelled to demonstrate mastery over things. They find pleasure in this. They want to show adults, other kids, and the world that they have knowledge and are good at things.

If you ever have known a 10-year-old, try to imagine his or her bedroom. Try to picture what is in it. Bedrooms are wonderful windows into the inner worlds of tweens and teens. When ethnographers have catalogued the contents of bedrooms of young tweens from different neighborhoods in different parts of the U.S., they find similar things, the same things you would have found in a 10-year-old's bedroom in the 1980's or the 1960's. They find:

- Trophies and certificates (i.e., symbols of accomplishment)
- Collections of dolls, baseball cards and other toys (i.e., examples of classified objects and organized knowledge)
- Stuffed animals from their younger years (i.e., transitional objects)

The bedroom of a teen is a different matter. Try to picture it. If you were able to see under the piles of clothes and discarded junk food wrappers, you would see a new emphasis on appearance. Grooming products, clothing and accessories become more prominent, as do images of aspirational people, like rock stars, athletes and other celebrities. The trophies and collections still exist, but are relegated to less important spaces of the bedroom. Things that were the focus of the bedroom are now reminders of their younger years, the new transitional objects. Again, the clothing styles, accessories and celebrities may have changed, but these are the same things you have found in the bedroom of a 15-year-old in the 1950's or the 1970's. Kids are kids.

This change in the contents of their bedrooms indicates a developmental change in their inner worlds. Teens, with the ability to think purely abstractly, start to use this new capacity, this new ability, to reason realistically about their futures. They begin to ask the quintessential teen question: "Who am I?"

To answer this question, kids on the older end of the tween-to-teen developmental continuum look for models of success. They try to answer, "Who am I?" by looking for people—adults, friends, and celebrities—whom they may want to be. When a teen has identified a model of success, the teen tries to emulate that person. The teen will literally try that person on by adopting his or her style of dress, mannerism and speech. The teen is trying to see if the person they have identified as a model of success fits, much the same way we try on a coat to see if it fits.

If you have teens in your own life, the evidence for this should be clear. Consider how often, how quickly and how radically their appearance changes. They are trying on different personae.

A problem for parents, educators, youth workers and industries that market to teens is trying to understand what causes a teen to chose one person as a model of success over another. It turns out to be idiosyncratic. Teens pick models based on their own values and perceptions of their own strengths and weaknesses.

HOW TWEENS AND TEENS LEARN

All kids have learning preferences; environments, methods and even instructor types that help them acquire and retain new skills and knowledge. The theories that describe and predict these preferences have evolved, but some theories from 80 years ago retain their validity. How kids want to learn has not changed over the years. Kids are kids.

That being said, learning preferences do change as kids journey across the tween-to-teen continuum.

The Tween-to-Teen Learning Preferences Continuum

Tweens ◀━━━━━━━━━▶ Teens	
⇨ Motivated by recognition of accomplishment	⇨ Motivated by successful individuals
⇨ Mimic behaviors of successful individuals	⇨ Mimic behaviors of successful individuals
⇨ Look for safe zones	⇨ Look for safe zones
⇨ Acquire the more difficult behavior with help and then repeat it	⇨ Acquire the more difficult behavior with help and then repeat it

Sources: Author's compilation.

Younger tweens, because they are naturally compelled to want to demonstrate that they have competence, are more likely to be motivated by recognition of accomplishment. They are motivated to learn if there is a chance to be recognized for learning.

In contrast, teens are motivated to learn by successful individuals. They are more likely to be interested in learning that they think will build this person that they are trying to be or model.

All kids want to learn by modeling. They want to watch somebody perform the task or demonstrate knowledge and then mimic the behavior of that person, repeating it until it becomes their own behavior.

Ideally, the person that kids want to learn from is somebody with whom they can identify, somebody who is a lot like they are. There are two main reasons for this. First, if you are a lot like me, for example, then there is a chance that we share the same language, which aids the communication of instructions and helps eliminate ambiguities. Second, if you are a lot like me then it is easier for me to imagine myself accomplishing whatever it is that I am about to attempt. Writing in the 1920's, the psychologist Lev Vygotsky called such instructors the More Knowledgeable Other or "MKO." Often the ideal MKO is a peer, another kid.

Kids want to experiment with learning. They want to be able to try to mimic the MKO in an environment where the consequences of failure are not so dire. Kids want to learn, to try new things, in safe zones. Kids need freedom to fail.

Kids are most comfortable learning that which is just at the limits of their reach. If it's too far away, if it's too hard to acquire the new knowledge or skill, then kids are likely to get frustrated and quit. Kids can know or do only what they are capable of knowing or doing. Conversely, if it is too easy, if it does not require them to extend or to apply all of what they have learned, then kids are likely to get bored.

Educational psychology uses the term "scaffolding," and I think it is a useful metaphor. Asking a kid to build the fourth floor of a building when the other three floors are not in place is setting the kid up for failure. Likewise, it would be tortuous to a kid to be asked to build the same first floor over and over again.

As you have been reading this, I hope you have been reflecting on your own childhood. Who in your own life taught you the most? Was it a teacher? A friend? A coach? Was it easy for you to master what they were teaching or did it take work? Did you fail initially? If so, what happened when you failed? Were you allowed to keep trying, or were you forced to quit? I hope that reflecting on these questions will help you recognize that how the current generation of young people want to learn is not that different from how you wanted to learn in your youth. Kids are kids.

HOW TWEENS AND TEENS
SPEND A TYPICAL DAY

We've looked at how tweens and teens are developing psychologically and how they want to learn. Now I would like to begin to examine their outer worlds; that is, what they do.

When I talk to groups of nonparents and ask them how tweens and teens spend their days, they tell me that the kids they know spend six hours each day playing videogames, another eight hours on the computer, at least 12 hours watching television, and an addition 16 hours text messaging. They claim that kids today are so technologically savvy that they are able use computers to bend the laws of physics just to spend more time online, watching TV and using mobile telephones.

When I talk to parents about their own children, a different phenomenon occurs. Parents often are reluctant to admit how much time their tweens and teens spend with media because they think it reflects poorly on them and their abilities to provide healthy, educational environments. I once conducted a focus group with parents of ten-year-old boys and girls and asked them how much television their children watch in a typical evening. The first mother said, "My son watches about one hour of television a night, and he only watches the Discovery Channel." The second mother said, "My son is allowed to watch a half hour a night, but only after his homework is done. He likes the History Channel." The third mother said, "My son watches fifteen minutes a night." It was all I could do not to follow up with, "Does he watch the first half of a program or the second half? Or maybe he maximizes his fifteen minutes by watching the last seven-and-a-half minutes of one program and the first seven-and-a-half minutes of the next program?"

The truth is that kids do spend a lot of time with media. The best research available indicates that a typical kid watches over four hours of television in a typical day. It also is true that kids spend more time with other media—like computers, mobile telephones and videogames—than ever before. However, as I mentioned at the beginning of this chapter, kids also spend significant portions of their days hanging out with friends and parents. They pursue hobbies, they play outdoors, and they even read. Even with the preponderance of new media, kids still find a way to be kids.

More important, how kids spend typical days fits who they are on the inside. Remember I said that as kids develop across the tween-to-teen continuum, they transition from a world of the home, where parents or caregivers and the immediate surroundings of their dwellings are the most important things to them, to a world of peers, where friends and the opinions of their cohorts become increasingly important. Therefore, it should not surprise you to see how much time typical kids spend on social activities. Hanging out with friends, playing with friends, communicating with them online and with telephones all occupy significant portions of their days. Although the gadgets and modes of communication may be new, younger tweens spend their days learning what it means to be autonomous individuals, separate from their parents, and older teens spend their days trying to figure out what kind of individuals they are. When we were kids, we did too.

How a Typical Kid Spends a Typical Day

Activity	Time
Watching television content	4:29
Listening to music	2:31
Hanging out with parents	2:17
Hanging out with friends	2:16
In physical activity	1:46
Texting on a cell phone	1:35
Using a computer	1:29
Playing video games	1:13
Talking on phone	0:51
Doing homework	0:50
Reading	0:38

Sources: Kaiser Family Foundation (2005, 2010).

I want to return to television—the single most time-consuming activity in typical day of a typical kid—and examine what tweens and teens are watching. When children hit the tween years, they typically stop watching cartoons and start watching live-action programs. Although the titles have changed, with one notable exception the most popular programs for tweens and younger teens for the last several years share many characteristics:

- The main character is a teen
- The plots revolve around the main character attempting to overcome a typical teen problem (e.g., pleasing a parent, dealing with gossip, succeeding at school, etc.)

- The main character has a fantastic quality (e.g., magical powers, extreme wealth, a secret identity, fame, etc.) that helps him or her ultimately resolve the problem after their initial attempts fail

Whether intentional or not, the fantastic qualities that the main characters in these popular programs share allow them to fail without dire consequences. Tween and young teen viewers get to live vicariously through these young main characters and explore from a safe distance those things that concern them most, namely being competent in the social world around them and discovering who they are as individuals.

The main characters of successful shows for this age range share other characteristics as well. First, they have successful peer relationships, which, as we have seen, is very important to tweens and teens. Second, they are quirky. They are good looking, but they are not fashion models. They are liked, but not necessarily the most popular kids. They are portrayed as competent, but not necessarily the best students or athletes or performers. As MKOs, those individuals that kids want to learn from, they are ideal: aspirational enough to capture a young viewer's attention but not so perfect as to seem unattainable.

Tweens and teens today are watching a lot of television. So were kids ten years ago, and twenty years ago, and even thirty years ago. When we look at what they watch and why they watch what they watch, we see that they are watching new and different shows, but for reasons that are timeless. We see that kids are kids.

WHY THEY SEEM DIFFERENT

When I talk to adults about tweens and teens, somebody invariably raises the objection that tweens and teens today "seem so much older." This is a legitimate observation. I believe there are two factors at play. The first factor is popular media's portrayal of tweens and teens. The second factor is a shift in adult behaviors.

The world of tweens and teens as portrayed by popular media often is very different from their actual world. If we view tweens and teens through this lens, then they may appear older. The consequence

Earlier Onset of Puberty in Girls

The much-publicized trend of girls developing certain signs of puberty earlier is true. This early onset of some secondary sexual characteristics seems linked to nutrition, and by that I mean food. Girls in developed nations have greater access to food today than in previous centuries. Although the exact relationship is not understood entirely, when a female's caloric needs are consistently surpassed, it signals her brain that she is capable of supporting a child. The result is an earlier onset of breast development, in particular.

However, the link between breast development and cognitive development is not one to one. The brain has not caught up to the body. The consequences for girls are particularly troubling.

Because they look older, girls who develop earlier may be treated as older and subjected to pressures they are not prepared to handle emotionally. These girls are more likely to use drugs, be sexually active and have trouble in school.

of this misinformation is harmful because it places a barrier between us, as adults, and the kids in our lives.

Here is a small example of how popular media can distort our view of the tweens and teens in our lives, one that we will return to later in this book. A few years ago, a popular talk show did an episode on online sexual harassment of female tweens and teens. The individuals interviewed for the program and the anecdotal evidence presented in the program implied that all young females who use social networking Web sites, like Facebook or MySpace, are constantly inundated with sexually explicit messages from rapists and molesters who are attempting to lure them to their demise. The program concluded by asking viewers to get involved in a grassroots effort to enact new federal legislation to prevent and punish online sexual harassment.

Coincidentally, *Pediatrics*, the official journal of the American Academy of Pediatrics, during the same time period published a comprehensive review of the data on sexual harassment in social networking Web sites and concluded, "Broad claims of victimization risk, at least as defined as unwanted sexual solicitation or harassment, associated with social networking sites do not seem justified" (Ybarra & Mitchell, 2008, p.350). The article went on to state, "Prevention efforts may have a greater impact if they focus on the psychosocial problems of youth instead of a specific Internet application."

To further illustrate the point, my company, New Amsterdam Consulting, and azTeen Magazine surveyed over 500 teenage females in Phoenix, Arizona, and asked them about sexual harassment in person as well as online. Respondents were twice as likely to be harassed at their schools, at their jobs and at the mall than they were online.

If adults base their understanding of kids on the images promoted by popular media, then there is the chance that the kids they know would appear deceitful when they say that they are not being sexually harassed online. This leads to mistrust, and mistrust destroys relationships. Furthermore, the hypersexualized youth in the media stories certainly seem older because of the adult situations they are portrayed as facing. However, as I have demonstrated, these kids are kids, and to treat them otherwise is to saddle them with responsibility that they are not developmentally prepared to handle.

In addition to the misleading images presented by popular media, shifts in adult behavior have contributed to this perception that tweens and teens are somehow "older" than they were in previous generations.

For example, parenting experts have noted a shift in parenting styles from a more autocratic parenting style to a more cooperative one. Instead of dictating decisions, the trend is for parents to involve their tweens and teens in the decision-making process. As a result, these tweens and teens seem "older" because the adults in their lives are treating them as if they were older, but treating a child as an adult does make her or him an adult. Kids are kids.

Researchers also are examining the phenomena of parents encouraging their children to behave more like them and of parents behaving more like children. Parents are treating their children like peers. The blending of kid and adult fashions and the fact that adults are hitting the traditional milestones of adulthood (e.g., marriage, home ownership, parenting, etc.) later and later in life illustrates how parents are behaving more like their children. The lines have been blurred.

Parents are behaving a little more like kids, which makes the kids seem a little more like adults, but treating them as peers and wearing the same clothes as them does not magically grant tweens and teens the internal capacities of adults. Inside, kids are kids.

WHAT ACTUALLY IS DIFFERENT

Kids are kids, but there are ways in which the world of today's tweens and teens differs from the world of prior generations. One is their unparalleled access to media. Forty years ago, 70 percent of the households in the United States had televisions, and those televisions received very few channels. Today, 68 percent of 11- to 14-year-old kids have televisions in their own rooms, 38 percent receive cable or satellite channels in their own rooms, and 21 percent receive premium cable or satellite channels like HBO or Showtime in their own rooms.

Forty years ago, Honeywell marketed the first-ever home computer. Called the "Kitchen Computer," it was offered in the Neiman Marcus catalog for $10,000. Today, 31 percent of 11- to 14-year-old kids have computers in their own rooms, and 21 percent have Internet access in their rooms.

In 1973, Dr. Martin Cooper invented the first mobile telephone, but the first commercial wireless call would not be made for another decade. Today, over 26 percent of 8 to 12-year-old kids have their own mobile telephones.

The consequences of kids having this much access to media are poorly understood. Historically, it was thought that exposure to media detracted from academic performance and other activities. However, more recent studies conclude that there is not a significant relationship between how much television kids watch, for example, and how well they do in school.

Likewise, time spent watching television or using computers does not seem to detract from relationships or other activities—quite the opposite, actually; it seems that the more time kids spend with media, the more engaged they are with the world around them.

Tweens and teens are able to consume so much media because they multitask. They text while they watch television, they listen to music while they play videogames, and they chat online while doing homework. While there is some research that suggests that multitasking like this means that tweens and teens comprehend less and are less able to respond to stimuli outside of those media (e.g., they are less likely to respond when a parent asks them a question, etc.), national statistics on reading and mathematics seem unaffected by this new co-use of media. In fact, mathematics and reading scores for 13-year-olds have improved slightly over the last 30 years.

Like it or not, we live in a world with hundreds of television channels and millions of Web sites. It is a world where the best, most reliable information about events has come in text messages from a cell phone, and careers and reputations are ruined by comments hastily posted to a blog. According to some academics, understanding this and being a part of it constitutes a new kind of literacy. In other words, kids who are not using computers and who are not exposed to television are not keeping up with the times. Tweens and teens who are savvy consumers of television, of the Internet and of mobile information are using skills that are necessary to succeed in our modern world. In some ways, these kids are the most literate.

It is a mistake to say that tweens and teens today are inherently different from adults or from prior generations of kids because of their media consumption. Adults also are consuming more media than ever before. All one has to do is observe fellow diners at a restaurant and see how often they check their mobile devices. Likewise, it is impossible to predict accurately how prior generations would have behaved if they had access to as much media as the current generation. Personally, I believe they would behave exactly as today's tweens and teens do.

The second major way in which today's tweens and teens differ from prior generations is their importance as consumers. Tweens, by themselves and out of their own pocket, spend an estimated $50 billion a year in the United States.

Furthermore, the spending habits of kids seem less affected by the economic downturn than that of adults. Again, there are several factors at play. Parents seem to be insulating their kids from the economy, handing out spending money at rates comparable to the past. Also, tweens and teens continue to find employment and seem to have complete discretion over the money they earn. My own comprehensive study of teen females in Phoenix, Arizona, indicates that only 26% of respondents spent less in 2009 than in 2008 because of the recession, receiving less money from parents or job loss.

Female Teens, Spending in 2009 Relative to 2008

Sources: New Amsterdam Consulting/azTeen Magazine (2009).

More importantly, tweens and teens have more influence on household purchasing decisions than ever before. Because of their kids' technological prowess, parents consider their offspring to be experts in all things modern. As a result, parents tell us that they rely on the advice of their tweens and teens when deciding to purchase everything from food to, incredibly, automobiles. It is worth noting that the children themselves often do not know the influence that they have. In a recent study of Canadian families, 60 percent of surveyed parents say that their kids influenced the purchase of the family car.

In comparison, only 30 percent of the surveyed children—the actual children of the surveyed parents—said that they influenced the purchase.

As influencers of family purchases, tweens are estimated to be responsible for another $120 billion in spending in the United States. It is no wonder that we see so much advertising on television, online and in stores directed at tweens and teens. They are the ones deciding what most households buy. This is a significant way in which the world of today's tweens and teens differs from the world of prior generations.

WHERE ARE KIDS ALLOWED TO BE KIDS?

If kids are kids, then ask yourself, "Where are they allowed to be kids?"

Can they be kids at home? At home they increasingly are treated like their parents' peers, they are required to participate in household governance, and they are relied upon to offer advice on major household purchases.

Can they be kids at school? Let me offer the following anecdote.

As part of my graduate work, I was a mental health counselor in a public middle school in one of the poorest suburbs of Boston. In reality, very few of the kids on my caseload had mental health problems in any clinical sense; instead, teachers used the service to get students with behavior problems out of their hair for an hour or two a week.

One of the young males I was counseling was the undisputed alpha male of the school. At 14-years-old, David was over six feet tall. He was not awkward and skinny like some tall, post-adolescent males; instead, David was built like an adult, a very muscular adult. Although he was loosely affiliated with his housing project's notorious, drug-dealing gang, David was polite, quiet and generally well liked by students, faculty and staff.

David was referred to counseling because he acted out in class. When I met with his teacher to discuss the details, this tiny woman, who was barely five feet tall, admitted to be being perplexed. She said,

"I asked him to do a problem on the blackboard, and he refused, which is not like David. When I asked him again, he stood up suddenly and threw his desk."

Although she hated admitting it, this teacher felt threatened. Her classroom had ceased to be a safe place for her. What she did not recognize was that, at that moment, her classroom ceased to be a safe place for David.

Kids want to learn in environments where they can model behaviors, where they can keep trying and failing until they learn the lesson, and where the consequences of failure are low. Furthermore, as kids age through the tween-to-teen developmental continuum, the opinions of their peers become increasingly important.

The consequences of making a mistake at the blackboard in front of a classroom of peers were frightening to David. The school was not teaching him in a manner consistent with how he innately wanted to learn, nor was it sensitive to his developmental needs. Developmentally, David was trying to formulate and project the image of the person he thinks he wants to be, and he was just ordered to jeopardize that image in front of his peers. If he makes a mistake, he does not get to try again. For David and many like him, schools are not places where kids can be kids.

If kids cannot be kids at home, and if kids cannot be kids at school, where can they be kids? In the world of videogames for one. Videogames are built to match how tweens and teens learn. For one thing, they scaffold. To progress through levels, players must use all of the skills they have and develop news ones. Videogames get harder as players get better at playing, and they get harder gradually so that each goal is that right distance away, neither too easy and boring nor too difficult and frustrating.

Videogames also offer immediate feedback on performance, rewarding demonstrated competence with points, stars, new levels and the like.

Unlike schools, the consequences of failing within videogames are temporary. If a player experiments and fails in a videogame, that player gets a new life or gets to start over. The slate is wiped clean.

Kids also are allowed to be kids online.

Several years ago, a giant media company asked me, "What's up with MySpace?" Kids comprised a significant user group, and I was hired to find out why tweens and teens were attracted to it. As a researcher, I did what researchers do: I looked for data, I read studies, and I interviewed users. What I learned explained the popularity of MySpace among kids and of social networks in general.

At the time, the typical young MySpace user was thought to have multiple profiles on average. In each profile, she or he was a different persona with different interests and different friends. By itself, that information might seem strange, may even indicative of a dissociative disorder. However, if you understand the developmental challenges of adolescence, then that behavior and the appeal of social networks start to make sense. These teen MySpace members were using their various profiles to test different models of success. They literally were trying on different personae to see which fit.

As I have explained, emulating different models of success comes naturally to tweens and teens, but other environments are less forgiving of this behavior. At school, classmates tend to be critical of one's attempts to change or to define oneself in a new way. Consider your own educational experience. Did you have a classmate whose reputation was forever marred by a public misstep? By wearing a different style? By embracing a different point of view?

Jake Tussing's high school experience in the 2008 documentary "American Teen" is a perfect example of this. Jake, a self-described recluse, credits his own lack of popularity to one event in middle school:

> I wasn't a shy kid, but then middle school started. In 7th and 8th grade, I was really tiny, so everyone, like, made fun of me all of the time for being short. One time, somebody knocked a bowl of hot chili all over my lap. I had to walk up in front of the whole school and ask if I could change my pants, and Nate Sarsgood was like, "Look everybody. Jakey got his first period." So everyone laughed. And that was pretty much, like, the point where, like, my life turned completely different. It shaped who I was going to be in high school. I think that's what made me be so afraid of who I am.

Jake's is an extreme example, and it is not about modeling a new persona, but it illustrates the consequences of failure in a school setting.

This is why kids flocked to MySpace and why they continue to use social networks. Kids perceive the consequences of failure to be less dire in social networks. They believe that social networks offer a safe place to work through development issues—like figuring out who one is by trying on different personae—in an environment where the cost of failure is less dear.

3

Kids Are Good

Several years ago, I was presenting to a group of children's television executives on the habits of their target audience. I addressed issues like the television programs kids watch, the videogames kids play, how kids spend their free time and so forth. Afterwards, a member from the audience came up to me and asked if I was familiar with new research linking "all of the problems with kids today" to texting.

I knew I would be entering into a "Kids These Days" discussion if I did anything but nod politely, but I could not help myself. "All of what problems?" I asked. "You know," she continued, "the sex and the drugs."

It is fascinating how many people, including individuals whose professions require them to pay attention to the behaviors and preferences of children and adolescents, assume that kids today are more nefarious, more depraved, and morally inferior than we adults were at their age.

I was fortunate to work with Neil Howe on a study of generational differences in perceptions of humor. Neil is the preeminent expert on generational differences, he and his partner, William Straus, authored several best selling books on the topic, and they even coined the term "millennial" to describe the generation of people born between 1982 and 2004. I called Neil and asked him about this repeating cycle of adults mistrusting kids and considering them to be morally inferior. Neil's initial response to me was, "You know, repetition doesn't necessarily automatically bring about correction. There are all kinds of cycles in nature that keep repeating, including cycles involving society and human beings."

Neil explained adults' attitudes towards kids this way:

> The young are trying to become adults. They're trying to gain power. They're trying to get to the top of the pecking order and control the herd, and the old bulls want to keep them down. I think in the context of human society, if you are older there's always a little bit of fear and jealousy of the young. They have time on their side. Their power and capabilities are mounting daily whereas yours are not, and I think that that goes on at a personal level. I think at a collective level there is always a desire among older people to demonstrate or defend the proposition that their values, their capabilities, are actually pretty worthwhile after all, and maybe the young's aren't all that worthwhile after all.

In the previous chapter I worked hard to convince you that kids are kids, that children and adolescents today are not that different than we were when we were their age, that their needs, desires, and even their educational preferences are very similar to what ours were when we adults were their age.

Neil's take on this is different. He sees generational differences that may make the worldviews of adults and kids fundamentally different.

> By generational differences, I mean those values and attitudes which are associated not just with the young versus the old, but are associated with that particular group of people who are young and old, who are shaped that way because of their location and history. I think that you find that in more modern societies history shapes people differently in enduring ways, and tradition doesn't force everyone back into conformity with the timeless norms.

In addition to changes to their external worlds, such as the media and technologies that are available to them, there is something else that is different about kids today, something that makes them different that we adults were at their age. Kids are good.

In almost every way that society cares about, kids today are better than kids were 10 years ago, 20 years ago, or even 30 years ago. In other words, kids today are better than we adults were at their age.

Don't believe me?

In this chapter, we will explore the different categories of behaviors that society seems most concerned about when it thinks about the health and well-being of children and adolescents:

- Sex
- Pregnancy
- Drug use
- Deliquency

SEX

As all things do, we will start with sex. What I am about to tell you is so shocking, so counterintuitive that you actually can use it to win a friendly wager at bar. I should know. A colleague of mine won a round of drinks off of me with this very same information. Kids today are having less sex than they were 10 years ago, than they were 20 years ago. In 1988, 51% of never-married female teens had ever had sexual intercourse. By 2002, that number had dropped to 46%. Interviews conducted by the Centers for Disease Control and Prevention (CDC) from 2006 to 2010 reveal that the number has dropped even lower. The CDC's most recent research indicates that only 43% of never-married females between the ages of 15 and 19 had ever had sexual intercourse.

During the same period, never-married males between the ages of 15 and 19 also were getting less and less "freaky." In 1988, 60% of male teens had ever had sexual intercourse. Like their female counterparts, the proportion of male teens who ever had sexual intercourse dropped to 46% in 2002 and, according to the most recent numbers from the CDC, 42% of never-married males between the ages of 15 and 19 had ever had sexual intercourse. That's right. Female high school students now are slightly more likely to have had sexual intercourse than male high school students.

Never-Married Teens, Age 15–19, Who Have Ever Had Sexual Intercourse

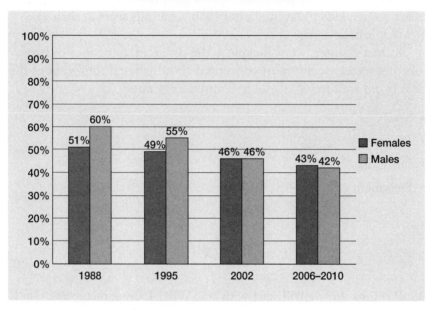

Source: Centers for Disease Control and Prevention (2011).

If you were like me, you find this almost unbelievable. Surely the amount of sexually explicit content in movies and on television and the overwhelming and seemingly omnipresent amount of pornography on the Internet is having some impact on kids. Perhaps we are looking at this the wrong way. Perhaps more and more kids are abstaining, but the ones who are not must be going crazy, right? I am talking Caligula meets Season 4 of *Nip/Tuck*, right? Wrong.

Kids are good.

Not only are fewer high school students having sexual intercourse, but the ones who are having sexual intercourse are having it with fewer and fewer partners. In 1991, 19% of high school students had sexual intercourse with four or more individuals in the course of their young lives. By 2009, that number had dropped to 14%.

Percent of High School Students Who Have Had Sexual Intercourse With Four or More Persons

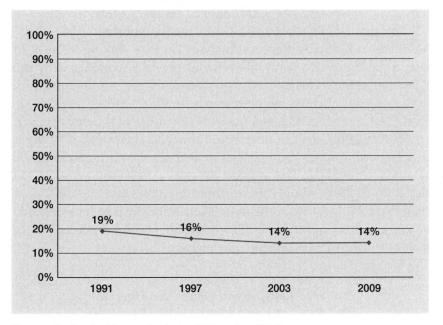

Source: Centers for Disease Control and Prevention (2011).

I recently shared this information with a group of school administrators. The cognitive dissonance was palpable. Then I witnessed a light bulb spark above the head of one very bright principal. "Yes," she said, "But aren't kids today substituting other kinds of sex for vaginal intercourse?" She was referring to the highly publicized research that came out of the Bradley Hasbro Children's Research Center in 2008.

From 1998 to 2002, researchers from the Bradley Hasbro Children's Research Center collected data from 1,348 participants of Project SHIELD, an HIV prevention program that targets 15- to 21-year-olds who have had unprotected sex in the past 90 days. The study found that risk factors like having two or more sexual partners and having been forced to have sexual intercourse were correlated with females engaging in anal intercourse. Likewise, the study found that sexual orientation, being gay, was correlated with males engaging in anal intercourse. The study was a snapshot of subset of at-risk youth during a given period of time. It did not address general trends.

But that is not what mainstream media reported. ABC News' headline read, "Study Reports Anal Sex on Rise Among Teens." In fact, a representative study of youth in the U.S. conducted by the CDC found little change in the prevalence of anal sex among youth in the six years covered by the research. In 2002, 20% of females age 15 to 24 had engaged in anal sex with a member of the opposite sex. In 2006 to 2008, that number stayed the same. Likewise, 22% of 15- to 24-year-old males had engaged in anal sex with a member of the opposite sex in 2002. That number dropped ever-so-slightly to 21% in the 2006 to 2008 study. It is worth noting that these numbers skew such that the older one is, the more likely he or she is to have engaged in anal sex. In the 2006 to 2008 study, only 7% of females and 6% of males age 15 to 17 had engaged in anal sex.

Percent of Youth, Aged 15 to 24, Who Have Ever Had Anal Sex with a Member of the Opposite Sex

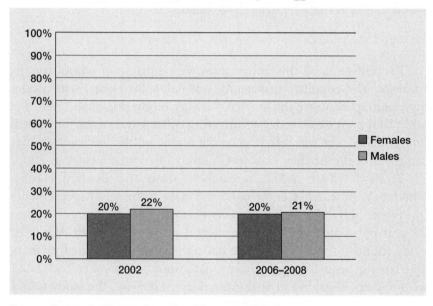

Source: Centers for Disease Control and Prevention (2011).

It also is worth noting that the percentage of kids having oral sex is declining. In 2002, approximately 69% of females, age 15 to 24, and 69% of males, age 15 to 24, had either given oral sex to or received oral sex from a member of the opposite sex at any time in their lives. Among the youth interviewed in the 2006 to 2008 study, 63% of females and 64% of males, age 15 to 24, had either given or received oral sex. Once again, the likelihood of having oral sex increases with age. In the 2006 to 2008 study, 30% of females, age 15 to 17, and 35% of males, age 15 to 17, had engaged in oral sex with a member of the opposite sex.

Percent of Youth, Aged 15–24, Who Have Had
Oral Sex with a Member of the Opposite Sex

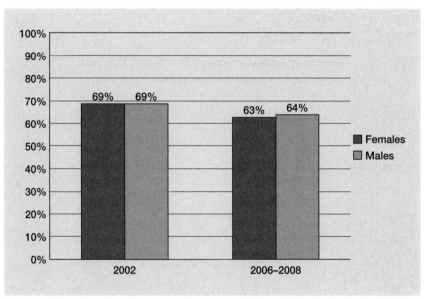

Source: Centers for Disease Control and Prevention (2011).

It's incredible, and I agree that it is more than reasonable to assume that easy access to sexually explicit information would somehow make our kids, our tweens and teens, more prone to having sex, but it simply is not the case. Researchers aren't always sure about why this is. There is a body of research that suggests that open access to information is demystifying or removing taboos of sex and sexuality, and that has resulted in less experimentation. Regardless, parents and other adults should rest assured that the kids in their lives are having less sex than we were at their age.

However, my point about kids being good is about more than the amount of sex and the types of sex kids are having. I argue that the thoughtfulness with which kids are approaching sexual intercourse is the best evidence that kids today are good. As I have demonstrated, more and more kids are abstaining from sex during their high school years. Just as important, I believe, is that the fact that those kids who are having sex are more likely than ever before to practice safe sex. In 1991, only 46% of high school students who were having sex used a condom during their last encounter. By 2009, that number had risen to 61%. That rate is not ideal, but as a percentage increase, it marks a huge improvement.

Percent of Sexually Active High School Students
Who Used a Condom During Last Intercourse

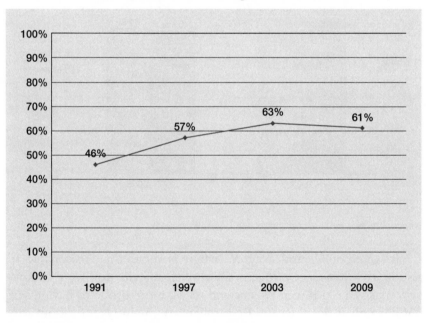

Source: Centers for Disease Control and Prevention (2011).

With this increased thoughtfulness has come a decrease in the teen birth rate. Fewer kids are having kids. In 2000, 48 out of every 1,000 females, age 15 to 19, gave birth to a child. By 2009, that number had dropped 19%. In 2009, a child was born to 39 out of every 1,000 females, age 15 to 19. Again, this rate may not be ideal, but a 19% decrease is a step in, what many of us believe is, a positive direction.

Live Births Per 1,000 Females,
Aged 15–19

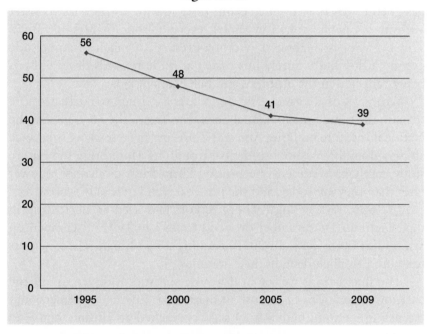

Source: Centers for Disease Control and Prevention (2011).

What do we do with this information? We'll discuss that later in this book. However, I want you to keep this in mind the next time you hear a morning show host describe some act of sexual depravity as the new trend among today's young people.

SUBSTANCE ABUSE

While we needn't worry quite as much about teenage pregnancy or sexual depravity, at least we can worry about our kids taking drugs, right? With the rise of marijuana dispensaries and depictions of substance abuse in mainstream media, surely our kids are using drugs at a greater rate, right? I mean, remember how freaked out we were when we watched Alex P. Keaton, who was so masterfully portrayed in *Family Ties* by Michael J. Fox, get hooked on the amphetamines his sister Mallory procured from her overweight friend, Effie? It was a "special" episode of *Family Ties*, it was advertised as such, and it was designed to teach us a valuable anti-drug lesson. Today, Molly's sister Victoria is openly stoned in almost every episode of *Mike & Molly*. This behavior is celebrated. Victoria even spent much of an episode getting a dog high. Surely this casual attitude towards drug abuse is being reflected in the attitudes and behaviors of kids.

Wrong. Kids are good. The trend lines for drug use fluctuate more than do the trend lines for sexual behaviors, but in the 36 years that the National Institute on Drug Abuse (NIDA) has been tracking substance abuse among high school students through its Monitoring the Future study, rarely have students been using illicit drugs or alcohol at lower rates than they are today, and the ten-year trend generally is positive.

In 1980, 65% of high school seniors had used an illicit drug in their lifetime. That number dropped to 48% in 1991. It climbed up again in 2000 to 54%. In 2010, roughly 48% of high school seniors have used an illicit drug in their lifetimes.

The fluctuations we see in drug use statistics is driven, in a large part, by fluctuations in the use of marijuana. Lifetime marijuana and hashish use among high school seniors reached an all-time high (no pun intended) in 1979, with 60% of high school seniors reporting that they had used marijuana at least once in their lifetimes. In 1992, the rate of marijuana use among high school students was the lowest, with only 33% of seniors reporting lifetime use. In 2010, 44% of high school seniors reported using marijuana or hashish in their lifetimes, which is down from 49% in 2000. Many researchers blame these fluctuations in marijuana use on kids' perceptions of the dangers of marijuana, which also have fluctuated.

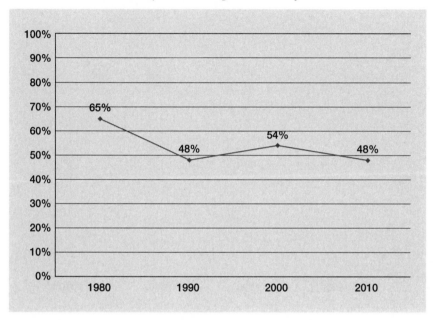

*Percentage of High School Seniors Who Have
Used Any Illicit Drug in Their Lifetime*

Source: National Institute on Drug Abuse (2011).

Methamphetamines are terrifying, or, at least, the public service announcements about meth are. The images from the various meth prevention campaigns are raw and shocking. The one that haunts me the most is a print ad from The Meth Project. It depicts a young, glassy-eyed female lying on her stomach under, what looks to be, a much older, deranged lumberjack. Its caption is, "15 bucks for sex isn't normal. But on meth it is." Haunting, right? Ads like this offer graphic depictions of the very real meth problem facing our kids.

Or do they?

In the 12 years that Monitoring the Future has tracked meth use among high school students, the percentage of high school seniors who have ever tried meth has dropped from 8% in 1999 to 2% in 2011. Much of that decline occurred prior to 2005. Moreover, the percentage of high school seniors who had used meth in the 12 months prior to the 2010 study is 1%.

Percent of High School Seniors Who Have Used Marijuana or Hashish in Their Lifetime

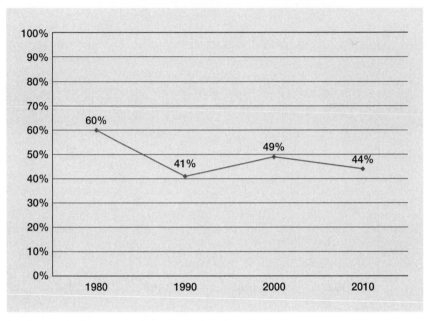

Source: National Institute on Drug Abuse (2011).

Please understand, in both my professional and my philanthropic work, I have labored to stop kids from using all illicit drugs, including meth. However, the meth "epidemic" does not appear to be an epidemic at all. If we were to believe the advertisements, we would assume that a large percentage of our kids are using meth. We would assume that kids today are not good, or, at least, that they were engaging in more dangerous behaviors than kids were 10 or 20 years ago. We might also assume they are high and lying about it. Misinformation creates barriers to real and meaningful communication between and adults and kids. This is why I want to debunk the meth myth.

Kids do drink alcohol. Alcohol is by far the most used drug among high school students. In 2010, 71% of high school seniors indicated

**Percent of High School Seniors Who Have
Used Meth in Their Lifetime**

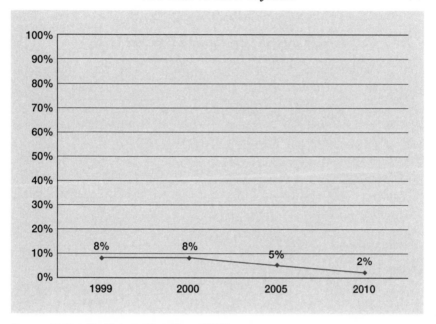

Source: National Institute on Drug Abuse (2011).

that they had used alcohol in their lifetimes. In 2010, 23% of high school seniors admitted to having five or more drinks in a row at least once in the two weeks prior to the study.

That level of alcohol use seems alarmingly high. To gain a better perspective on this number, let's look at use of alcohol by 35-year-olds during the same period. In 2010, 96% of 35-year-olds said they had tried alcohol at least once in their lifetimes, 23% of them reported having five or more drinks in a row at least once in the two weeks prior to the study. It turns out that high school seniors and 35-year-olds binge drink at the same rate, which is something you might want to keep in mind before you begin a "Kids These Days" rant.

Moreover, lifetime alcohol use among high school seniors is at an all-time low. The current rate of 71% of high school seniors having tried alcohol in their lifetimes is 25% lower than it was at its all-time high in 1980, when 93% of high school seniors had tried alcohol in their lifetimes.

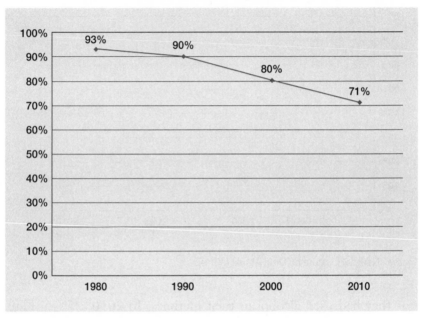

Percent of High School Seniors Who Have Used
Alcohol in Their Lifetime

Source: National Institute on Drug Abuse (2011).

If we take a closer look at how substance abuse is portrayed in the media, we notice that the people who are smoking marijuana are not kids. They are adults. Perhaps it is not surprising, therefore, that adults, trends in marijuana use sometimes appear more troubling than kids' trends. For example, in 2000, roughly 6% of high school seniors reported using marijuana every day. In 2010, the rate was essentially unchanged, at 6%. In 2000, 3% of 35-year-olds reported using marijuana daily. By 2010, that number had risen to 4%. As I mentioned, statistics on marijuana use fluctuate, and this statistic about 35-year-olds may be anomalous. I present it to make a point. Before we, as adults, engage in "Kids These Days" talk, maybe we should examine our own behaviors. Kids are good. Are adults?

Percent High School Seniors and 35-Year-Olds
Who Currently Use Marijuana or Hashish Daily

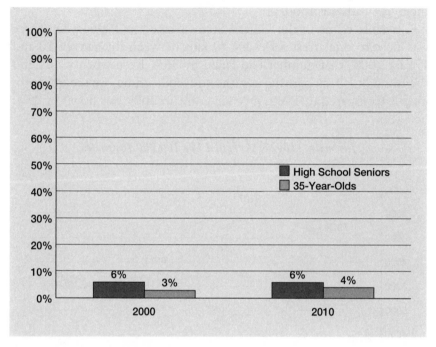

Source: Centers for Disease Control and Prevention (2011).

CRIME AND DELINQUENCY

"Sure," you might say, "kids aren't abusing substances and they aren't sexually promiscuous, but they are more delinquent, more violent than we were their age." You might cite as proof the amount of violence on television and in popular music, and the American Academy of Child and Adolescent Psychiatry's warning that these things have a negative impact on kids' behaviors. You might point to the number of school shootings in recent year. You might even note that even Brangelina—the most famous and, therefore, the best parents in the world—have violent and unruly kids according to their "friends" interviewed by Hollywood Life. If Brangelina have violent and unruly kids, all of us must have them as well.

Not so.

In almost every category tracked by the U.S. Justice Department, kids are committing fewer crimes than we adults did when we were their age. Kids are good.

Juvenile crime in the United States peaked in 1996, when there was close to one arrest for every 10 kids between the ages of 10 and 17. By 2009, that number had fallen by 36%. Even when we extend the trend line back past the zenith of juvenile crime, we see improvements. Compared to 1989, juvenile crime in 2009 was down by 27%.

Juveniles (10–17) Arrested Per 100,000 Juveniles

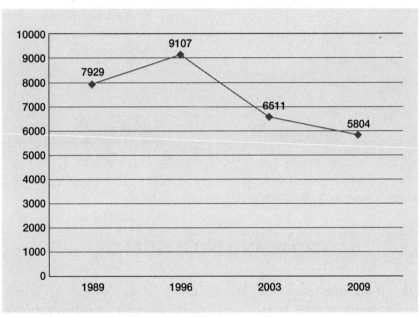

Source: National Center for Juvenile Justice (2011).

But crimes in general are not what cause us to cross the street when we see a group of teenagers walking towards us on the sidewalk. We are afraid of violent crimes; crimes like murder, non-negligent manslaughter, forcible rape, robbery, and aggravated assault. Luckily for us, violent crime also is down. In fact, the rate at which kids are committing violent crimes is the lowest it has been in 30 years. Between

1989 and 2009, the number of juveniles arrested for violent crimes fell by 32%. Between 1994, the most violent year on record, and 2009, the number of juveniles arrested for violent crimes fell by 47%.

Juveniles (10–17) Arrested for Violent Crimes
Per 100,000 Juveniles

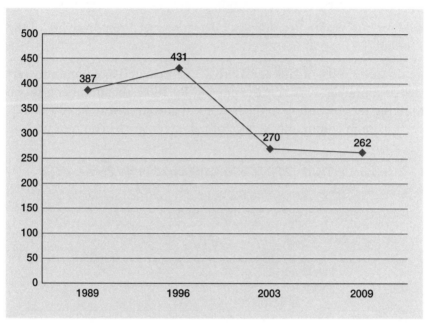

Source: National Center for Juvenile Justice (2011).

Kids aren't just good; they are getting better. And they are getting better faster than the rest of society. While the numbers of juveniles arrested for violent crimes fell by 13% from 2000 to 2009, the numbers of adults arrested fell by only 6% during the same period. Now, there are a few categories of crimes where adults are trending positively and at faster rates than juveniles, but they seem to be the exception. Besides, my point of presenting these numbers is to convince you that kids today are good and to combat the myths inherent in "Kids These Days" conversations.

GOOD BEHAVIORS

It isn't just the things that kids today *don't do* that make them good. Kids today are good because of things that they *do*. Kids today:

- Volunteer
- Are committed to the environment and their communities
- Make purchasing decisions based on the social responsibility of the brand

In 2003, 60% of kids age 12 to 17 participated in community service or volunteer work at least annually. By 2007, that number was one third higher. According to the best, most current research, 78% of kids participate in community service of volunteer work in a given year.

Percent of Youth (12–17) Who Volunteered in the Previous Year

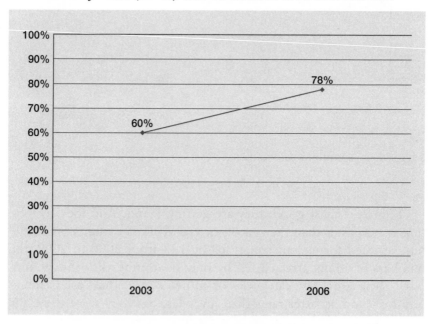

Source: Center for Child and Adolescent Health (2012).

Moreover, kids' commitment to community service appears strong. Among those kids who volunteer in a given year, almost half volunteer at least monthly.

Youth (12–17) Commitment to Volunteerism

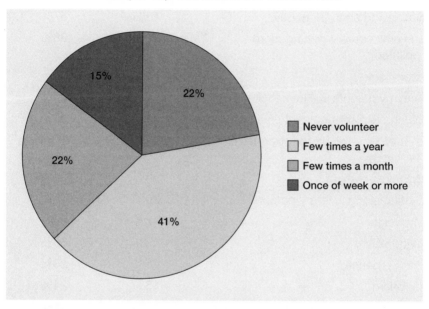

Source: Center for Child and Adolescent Health (2012).

This commitment to social causes and to their friends and family is evident in their expressed worries. Tweens worry more about the environment and the health and well-being of their friends and family than they do about their own appearances. Personal appearance and financial matters start to matter more to kids as they age across the tween-to-teen continuum, but the health and well-being of people close to them still concerns teens more than does their appearance or their romantic relationships.

Kids' (8–17) Worries

	8- TO 12-YEAR-OLDS	13- TO 17-YEAR-OLDS
Getting good grades in school	55%	60%
That someone close to me will get sick or die	50%	52%
Not having enough money	40%	57%
The environment getting more polluted	29%	38%
How I look	26%	44%
That my parents will lose their jobs	23%	26%
Getting in a car accident	21%	35%
That college will be too expensive for me	20%	50%
Being overweight	20%	34%
Getting along with my parents	20%	28%
My weight	17%	39%
Dying young	17%	36%
Getting cancer	15%	28%
Terrorism	15%	24%
That I won't find a boyfriend/girlfriend	12%	31%
None of these	8%	7%

Source: Harris Interactive (2010).

Finally, many studies by market research companies indicate that social responsibility is a brand attribute that kids pay attention to when deciding when and how to spend their own money. For example, a 2008 market research study by Just Kid Inc. found that kids are more likely to purchase products that support social causes than products that offer rewards to the purchaser.

Kids are good. We need to keep this in mind when we regard the kids in our lives. Knowing that kids are good will help debunk some of the myths about them. Moreover, knowing that they are good and committed to the community provides new topics of conversation and new avenues of communication. Knowing that kids are good also will help us believe the kids in our lives when they assure us that they are not doing the stupid things that we did when we were kids.

4

Kids Need Parents

Kids need parents. This may be my most obvious of claims. For one thing, kids need parents just to exist. We've known this to be true since humans stopped believing in spontaneous generation.

The definition of parent that I'm going to use entails more than providing DNA. An analysis of countless studies of the role of parents in raising healthy and successful kids reveals two defining characters of parents that are far more important than genetics. To be a parent, and individual must:

- Protect his or her children
- Teach his or her children

Kids need parents to protect them from hunger, physical harm, emotional harm, illness, and dangers of all sorts while they are still too small and too inexperienced to protect themselves.

While they are being protected, kids need parents to teach them how to protect themselves and how to be successful in obtaining and maintaining those things that humans needs, such as food, shelter and healthy relationships.

The protecting and teaching roles that are essential to parenting are interrelated. Often the teaching is occurring while the protection is being provided and, as mentioned, the teaching often is explicitly about protecting.

In this chapter, we are going to explore some of the ways that parenting impacts children. Later in the book, we will review strategies for successful parenting, especially as they relate to some modern issues facing our kids. However, before we get much further, recalling how kids learn is essential to understanding how parents teach. Kids learn by modeling behaviors. Consequently, what parents say often is much less important than what they do. This becomes obvious as we review the influence that parents have on kids.

Since we just finished a chapter on kids being good, let's start by looking at how parents influence desirable behaviors.

PARENTS AND SEX

In my company's survey of female youth in Arizona, parents ranked higher than any other group in a list of people who influenced respondents' decision to have sex. The list included friends, religious leaders and even celebrities. It is worth noting that in a world that is seemingly obsessed with the influence of celebrities, only 5% of the female youth surveyed indicated that celebrities influence their decision to have or not have sex.

Who Influences Young Females (12–21) in Their Decision to Have Sex

Parent	39%
Friend	34%
Religious leaders (priest, rabbi, pastor, minister, youth leader)	23%
Other	18%
Brother/sister	13%
Doctor/nurse	6%
Celebrities	5%
Teacher	5%
Coach	3%

Source: New Amsterdam Consulting/azTeen Magazine (2008).

The influence parents have over issues related to sex trumps many of the other factors that we, as adults, tend to worry about influencing kids. For example, the respondents to my survey indicated that their decision to have or not have sex was based more on their perceptions of the opinion of their parents than on peer pressure, media influence, celebrity role models, or even the influence of drugs or alcohol. Depending on how you interpret these respondents' views about religion and religious leaders, parents might be, to paraphrase John Lennon, more popular than Jesus. Whether or not that is the case, it is clear that kids need parents to educate them about sex and to protect them from negative sexual experiences.

What Influences Young Females (12–21) in Their Decision to Have Sex

Worried about getting pregnant	61%
Worried about getting a disease (STD, HIV, etc.)	52%
Waiting until marriage	50%
Worried parents would find out	34%
Religious reasons	32%
Worried I'd get caught	27%
Pressure from boyfriend/girlfriend	11%
Nothing, we do it all the time	9%
Alcohol	9%
Boyfriend/girlfriend isn't ready, said "no"	8%
Pressure from other friends	7%
What you see on TV/music videos	4%
Drugs	4%
What young celebrities do	3%

Source: New Amsterdam Consulting/azTeen Magazine (2008).

The Influence of Dancing Stars

Last year, Keith Ablow—a member of the Fox News Medical "A Team"—was encouraging parents to forbid their children to watch *Dancing with the Stars*. Keith believes it could be harmful for kids to see Chaz Bono celebrated as star. He is worried that children might believe that the answer to their insecurities is to do what Bono did and claim a different sexual identity.

I could not have disagreed more. At the time, I argued, and still do, that the presence of Bono on that program created a perfect opportunity for parents to interact with their children about sexuality, about courage, and about standing up for oneself, even when doing so is difficult or unpopular.

But am I being hypocritical? After all, I made a similar argument about Bristol Palin when she was on *Dancing with the Stars*. I argued that having Bristol on *Dancing with the Stars* sends a confusing message to vulnerable kids that might be interpreted as, "have an unplanned pregnancy as a teenager and you will be a star."

So why do I think that my recommendation and that of Keith are different?

Bristol freely chose to have unprotected sex. She may have been reacting to pressure, struggling under a lack of moral guidance, or experiencing issues with her self-esteem, but she made a choice. It is a choice that all adolescents are making or will need to make. Bristol's situation is relevant to all teens.

An impressionable teen could rush out and have unprotected sex in an attempt to emulate Bristol. In contrast, an impressionable teen cannot rush out and have sex reassignment surgery to emulate Chaz. The standard of care dictates multiple mental health assessments, intensive therapy, and extended "real life experience" living as the gender one identifies as.

Curiosity about the sex act is a normal part of adolescence, and so is, as Keith correctly stated at the time, insecurity about one's sexuality.

What is not normal is a long-term, strong and persistent identification with another gender and a long-term and persistent discontent with one's own biological sex or gender assignment. That is called "Gender Incongruence," and there is increasing scientific evidence that it is not a mental disorder, but a physical one that is successfully rectified with surgery (the *Diagnostic and Statistical Manual of Mental Disorders*, the authority on mental disorders, currently is revising its classification to account for these scientific findings).

As we ponder this, here are some questions you might have for both Keith and me:

Why didn't we object to Holly Madison as a *Dancing with the Stars* contestant? She is a star because she underwent breast augmentation to pose nude for Playboy. Should we worry about teens modeling Madison's behavior?

Why didn't we protest Kim Kardashian's appearance on the show? She was unknown until she made a sex tape with Ray J. What lesson can teens learn from her?

Finally, can't we both agree on a better TV program to recommend?

PARENTS AND SUBSTANCE ABUSE

In a famous Partnership for a Drug-Fee America public service announcement from 1987, a frizzy-haired, mustachioed father interrupts his teenage son, who is sprawled out on his bed with headphones on, rocking out. The father holds out a box of drug paraphernalia and says, "Is this yours? Your mother says she found it in your closet." The son tries to make excuses, but the father won't allow for it. Finally, the father asks, "Who taught you how to do this stuff?" The son breaks down. "You. All right?" the son says, "I learned it by watching you."

The PSA is often parodied, and one can watch it on YouTube, something I highly encourage, as it offers an interesting glimpse at life in the late 1980's. Moreover, the message is as timeless as it is true: Parents who abuse drugs and alcohol have kids who abuse drugs and alcohol.

Numerous studies document the importance of family history in predicting drug and alcohol abuse by kids. Many of them posit a biological link, suggesting that this cycle of parents who abuse substances raising kids who abuse substances who then raise their own kids who abuse substances implies a genetic proclivity to the abuse. However, the role of parents as protectors and teachers in this relationship is undeniably important.

More and more states are adjusting their definitions of child abuse and neglect to include exposure to a parents' substance abuse. The justification, based largely on solid research, is two-fold. First, substance abuse by parents marks failure in their roles as teachers. By their example, these parents are instructing their children that abusing substances is a viable way to get one's needs met. Second, the advocates of these newly amended definitions of child abuse and neglect argue that parents who abuse substances are absent as parents when they are under the influence. In other words, parents are not protecting their children when they are high.

As scary as this all seems, there is a body of research that promotes the flip side of the parents-who-abuse-drugs-have-kids-that-abuse-drugs coin. It is known as the Importance of Family Dinners research, and it comes out of The National Center on Addiction and Substance Abuse at Columbia University. The 2011 report demonstrates that teens who regularly eat dinner with their parents are less likely to abuse substances, are less likely to have friends who abuse substances, and are even less likely to know how to obtain drugs. This is just further proof of how much kids need parents, how mere exposure to parents protects kids and teaches them positive pathways to success.

Marijuana in the Lives of Teens (12–17)
by Frequency of Family Dinners

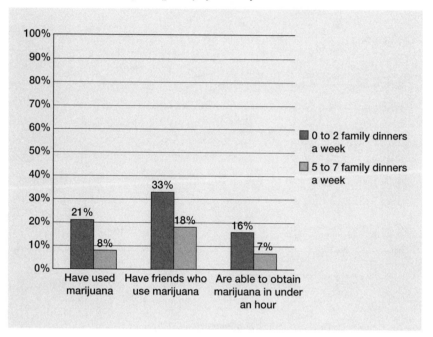

Source: National Center on Addiction and Substance Abuse at Columbia University (2011).

PARENTS AND OBESITY

I am very concerned about the weight of our kids. In the preceding chapter, I outlined many things that are trending in a positive direction for tweens and teens. Weight is not one of them. From the time childhood obesity entered the public conscience in the early 2000s, the percentage of kids who are obese has not gone down. In fact, from 1999 to 2009, the percentage of high school students who are obese actually increased. In 1999, 11% of high school students were obese. In 2009, 12% of high school students were obese.

**Percent High School Students Whose Body Mass
Index Is Above the 95th Percentile**

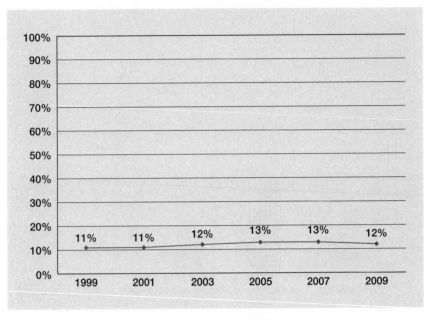

Source: Centers for Disease Control and Prevention (2011).

To give some idea of what it means for a kid to be obese, the typical 10-year-old male in the U.S. is 51 inches tall and weighs between 53 and 70 lbs. Obesity is defined as having a body mass index in the 95th percentile or above for one's age. An obese 10-year-old boy weighs more than 81 lbs at 51 inches tall. Consider what 10 extra lbs looks like on your frame. Now imagine what an extra 10 lbs looks like on a frame that is just over four feet tall. That is childhood obesity.

Obesity is just one of the reasons that kids need adults, but obesity serves as an important example because it highlights three different ways that kids need parents. To combat obesity, kids need parents to:

- Protect them from unhealthy food options
- Teach them about nutrition by modeling healthy eating habits
- Teach them about exercise by modeling a commitment to physical activity

Research also indicates that as kids spend less time with a parent, their obesity increases. Without parents, kids are more likely to be obese because, without a parent to protect them from unhealthy food options, kids are more likely to decide to eat the sugary or high-fat foods that are in so many of the commercials directed at kids.

Likewise, we parents can help our kids fight obesity by modeling healthy eating habits. Researchers say that this happens when parents eat meals with their kids and eat healthy foods during their meals. Again, kids need parents to teach them what to do by modeling the desired behaviors. It turns out that when parents coerce kids to eat a certain way or forbid certain foods without modeling the desired behavior, the long-term effect can be the opposite of what is intended, and kids can grow to dislike the foods they were forced to eat.

Finally, we know that physical fitness also is taught, and by "taught" I mean that kids need parents to model healthy exercise habits. In one study funded by the National Heart, Lung and Blood Institute, researchers found that children in two-parent households where one parent was active were at least twice as likely to be active compared to children in households where neither parent was active. In households where both parents were active, children were nearly six times more likely to be active than children in households where neither parent was active. Six times. At the risk of stating the obvious, that's a lot.

Sex, substance abuse and diet are just three examples of how kids need parents, how parents help their children be successful by protecting and teaching them. This parental influence is not limited to these three domains. Indeed, studies indicate that by protecting and teaching their kids, parents influence everything their kids do, from how much they volunteer to the types of music they like.

Finally, and this might be the most shocking of all the claims in this section, kids not only need parents; they want parents. Kids want to spend time with their parents and they want their parents to protect and teach them.

Impact of Physically Active Parents
on the Physical Activity Level of Children (4–7)
in Two-Parent Households

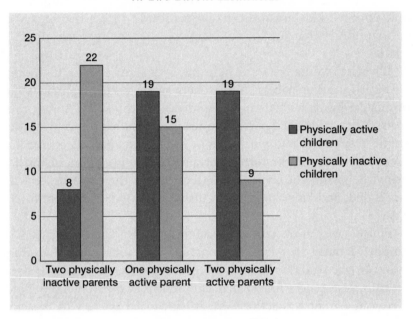

Source: Centers for Disease Control and Prevention (2011).

If you're still reading this after that last outlandish claim, you might be thinking, "Brad, my teen wants nothing to do with me. She doesn't even look at me. She just sits there, hunched over looking at her phone. If I ask her a question, she grunts in response." I acknowledge this behavior. I am witness to it in both my private and professional lives. However, we adults should not mistake the external appearance of the kids in our lives for their internal needs or desires.

In the 2008 New Amsterdam Consulting/azTeen Magazine survey of teenage females in Arizona, 20% of respondents indicated that they would be happier if they could spend more time with parents. A 2009 study by Harris Interactive indicated that tweens like spending time with their mothers more than they like spending time with their friends. Friends become more important as kids move through the tween-to-teen continuum, but Mom remains the one individual kids trust most.

Kids' Rankings of Important People in Their Lives

WHICH OF THE FOLLOWING PEOPLE . . . ?*	8- TO 12-YEAR-OLDS		13- TO 17-YEAR-OLDS	
	# 1 RESPONSE	# 2 RESPONSE	# 1 RESPONSE	# 2 RESPONSE
Would you call first in trouble	Mom	Dad	Mom	Dad
Do you trust the most	Mom	Dad	Mom	Friends
Understands you best	Mom	Dad	Friends	Mom
Can you talk most openly with	Mom	Dad	Friends	Mom
Do you most like to spend time with	Mom	Friends	Friends	Mom

*Possible responses included "Mom," "Dad," "Friends," and "Boy/Girl Friend."

Source: Harris Interactive (2009).

So kids need parents, and kids want parents, but being a parent is not easy. It takes skill to effectively protect and teach. In particular, I believe that there are three skills that parents must foster in order to effectively protect and teach children: presence, persistence and patience.

The Three Parenting Skills

The three skills parents need to develop to effectively protect and teach:

- Presence
- Persistence
- Patience

Actively being present in the lives of our kids helps us parents protect and teach of them. As mentioned, kids learn by modeling. They can model only behaviors that they see. If we want our kids to be a certain kind of human, then they must see us being that kind of human. They must be around us in order to see that, and we must be present to them.

We parents also need to be present to our kids to protect them. As we will discuss later in this book, as a society we have come to rely too much on mechanized protection. We look for alarms, filters and locks to keep harm away from our kids, but all of these things can be compromised. If we really want to protect our children from harmful images on television, for example, we need to be present to our children when they are watching television in order to see what they're watching, to talk to them about what they're watching, and to help explain to them what they're watching. If we want to protect our kids from cyberbullying and other online threats, for example, then we must be present to see what our kids are doing online. If we want to protect our kids from the wrong type of influence and from being with the wrong crowd, then we need to be present to our children when they're with their friends so that we can know who their friends are and what they do with their friends.

Why Your Kids Mistreat You In Front of Their Friends

"Brad, if my kid likes me so much, why does she treat me so differently when her friends are around? She seems to intentionally instigate arguments." It's a complaint I have heard from many parents. A common assumption for many parents in this situation is that kids act out in front friends because these kids believe that their parents will not react as forcibly if friends are around. From my work with kids, I believe opposite to be true. Often kids act out or instigate reactions from parents in front of friends precisely so that their friends can witness how protective their parents are. This can be a great asset for a kid if the kid ever finds herself without a parent or adult in a situation that she does not like. A kid with a parent who is well known for being strict can blame their unwillingness to do something (e.g., experiment with drugs or alcohol, ditch class, etc.) on that parent. She can say something like, "My mom would kill me if she ever found out, and she finds out everything."

Think back on your own experiences. Was there someone in your circle of friends who managed to avoid some of the more idiotic things the rest of us did because her parents were strict? What about the opposite? Growing up, did you know somebody whose parents did not care how late she stayed out or what she did? At the time, did you think her parents were cool? What sort of trouble did she get into? How do you feel about her parents now? The same dynamics that were at play then are at play now. Kids are kids, and kids need parents.

As parents, we need to let our kids scapegoat us. We need to be willing to be the bad guy in front of our kids' friends. Our kid's friends are not our friends. Our kids are not our friends either, for that matter. We are parents, and our job is to protect and teach.

Being present, like so many worthwhile skills, takes practice. Often we adults are so distracted by the very real responsibilities in our complicated lives that we forget how pleasurable it can be participate in the lives of our kids. To practice being present and to remind yourself of the joy that such presence can create, try the following techniques:

- Separate yourself from distractions like mobile telephones and e-mail
- Make eye contact

- Be close physically (e.g., if she is sitting down, sit down beside her, etc.)
- Allow yourself to be fascinated and amazed by the young human you are creating

We need to remember that being present is not standing in the doorway to our kid's room and asking her how school was as we scan e-mails on our iPhones.

Charles Duhigg, author of *The Power of Habit: Why We Do What We Do in Life and Business*, described his path to being present to his own kids in an interview with Terry Gross on Fresh Air this way:

> If I give you a piece of chocolate, your body recognizes that reward whether you even pay attention to chewing or not. But when it comes to emotional rewards or mental rewards, the only time you see the chemical, the neurological signature associated with pleasure and reward, is if the person stops and actually recognizes that they're enjoying this thing. And so that's what I'm working on right now, is recognizing the enjoyment that spending time with my kids or my wife gives me.

Persistence is another important parenting skill that is difficult to master. Like presence, persistence helps us parents with our dual role of protecting and with teaching. We all know that learning a new skill takes practice and repetition. We all wish that we could have the perfect golf swing the first time we tried. With something like golf, we resign ourselves to the fact that it is going to take a lot of repetition, a lot of persistence, to get it right. However, we get very frustrated as parents when we have to continually tell our children over and over again to do something. Being a parent is a lot like being a golfer: You spend a lot of money on something that is often infuriating, you think you are doing everything right but the results are all over the place, and alcohol makes it more enjoyable. Being a kid also is like being a golfer, minus the alcohol part. Kids need to practice desirable behaviors over and over again until they become second nature. Because our jobs are to protect and teach, we parents need to be persistent in order to foster success in our kids. We need to be persistent in our protection and persistent in our teaching.

Persistence has a very special meaning in that it describes a quality of something happening continually and consistently. Because children learn more by observing what we parents do than by listening to what we say, it is important to be persistent with the rules we set. The teaching and protection that are inherent in these rules we set sometimes are learned only when the rules are challenged or broken. We parents need to practice persistence so that we can consistently model and enforce the rules we set, so that we can remind our kids to clean up their rooms for the 1,000th time.

We parents also need to be persistent in questioning our kids about those aspects of their lives that we can't always be present to. While being present is very important, we parents can't be with them their entire school day, for example. We aren't always going to be with them when they are hanging out with friends. We can't always be present when our kids are watching TV, watching movies, listening to music, going online, or playing videogames. Consequently, we parents need to ask our kids about these things, and we need to ask them over and over again because the first time we ask a tween or teen a question about something, there's a very real possibility that we will not get an answer or the answer will be monosyllabic or even that the answer will be a primordial grunt.

From my time as a mental health counselor in the middle school, I can attest to the importance of persistence. More often than not kids who really want help from an adult will not ask for that help the first time that they are questioned. Persistence in questioning helps kids understand that the person asking those questions is indeed interested and that the kids' response would be valued.

It also is possible that we parents taught our kids that they must be asked multiple times before giving a response. Think back to when the kid in your life was 5 years old. How often were you focused on something important when that child asked, "Mommy?" How many times did your child say, "Mommy," before you responded? Did you always answer after the first, "Mommy"? Did it ever take a barrage of "Mommy! Mommy! Mommy! Mommy! Mommy!" before you finally snapped, "What?!" If you are a busy parent living a modern life, there is a good chance that this has happened to you. Your kids model your behavior. Remember this as you repeatedly ask the tween or teen in your life the same questions over and over again without a response. Remember this and be persistent.

Patience is the third P. From the examples in the discussions of presence and persistence, it should be obvious just how important patience is. For example, persistence often requires patience because it is hard to ask a kid the same question multiple times without receiving an answer. It is easier for us parents to believe that no answer is forthcoming than to ask a kid six times about her school day. If this were a friendship and a friend were treating us this way, we might walk away from that friendship, as it would be rude for a friend to treat our interest so coldly. But our relationship with our kids is not a friendship. Our relationship with our kids is parent and child, and it requires patience in order for us to be present and persistent.

We also have to be patient in our presence because, quite frankly, some of the things that interest our kids, things we have to be present to, are boring to us as adults. For example, typical television programs targeting a tweens or teens are mind numbing to adults. To us, the stories and the characters come across as saccharine and contrived. It requires all the patience that we can muster to sit through them, but being patient so that we can be present to what our kids watch on television eventually will pay off as we are better able to raise successful kids.

One reason we need patience while we are being present and persistent is because of precisely how much our opinions do matter to our children. The research on this is highlighted earlier. When our kids are facing something difficult, or when they have struggled and perhaps feel that they have failed, our patience, persistence and presence may be the only things that are going to allow them to ask for help.

As we will explore later in this book, bullying illustrates the importance of the three Ps rather well. Being bullied can be incredibly humiliating to kids. Many kids come to believe that they deserve the bullying and that, if they reveal the bullying to us as parents, then we as parents will think less of them. Consequently, kids may not reveal that they are being bullied the first time they are asked about it or the second time. They might wait until they are certain that our interest is real and that we will remain patient, persistent and present to them as we protect them and teach them how to resolve the situation.

5

Kids Need Adults

After spending my undergraduate years in the Phoenix area working in youth programs and trying to start a shelter for homeless and runaway teens, I headed to graduate school in New York City. One of my first jobs in New York City was coordinating a crime and delinquency prevention program that was operating in settlement houses across the New York City's five boroughs. The program was one of many Summer of Safety pilot programs for the newly formed Corporation for National and Community Service.

Kids in each location came together to serve their communities in ways that made their communities safer and, in doing so, these kids found purpose and the courage to persevere against the drugs and delinquent behaviors that were compromising so many of their peers in these very dangerous neighborhoods. I enjoyed the work immensely and might have continued at it for the rest of my life, if I weren't so curious about some of the dynamics that were hidden from me.

For every kid who volunteered to be a part of the program, there were numerous kids who did not. At the time, professionals who worked with and studied youth talked a lot about risk factors. Risk factors are characteristics that are associated drug abuse, poor academic performance, delinquency, etc. Risk factors include being poor, coming from a single-parent household, having delinquent peers, and coming from a high-crime neighborhood. The kids in the neighborhoods where we were running the Summer of Safety programs had all of these risk factors and more. So why then, I wondered, did some of the kids with all of these risk factors succeed while so many of the kids with the same risk factors fail?

At the time Harvard had a master's program in developmental psychology entitled Risk and Prevention. It seemed like an ideal opportunity to learn more about risk and resiliency, and I was thrilled when I was accepted. Each class, each reading, and each assignment was devoted to understanding the motivations of children and adolescents, particularly how they relate to behaviors such as criminal activity, drug abuse, and poor school performance.

One of the core classes for the degree was taught by my student advisor, Dr. Gil Noam. Gil undeniably is one of the foremost experts on child and adolescent development. As a faculty member at the Harvard Medical School and the Harvard Graduate School of Education, as a colleague of Erik Erikson, and as Founder and Director of the Program in Education, Afterschool and Resiliency, Gil has worked with and studied thousands of at-risk youth. That experience had yielded over 200 academic papers, articles and books. In short, when it comes to at-risk youth, Gil is the man.

On the very last day of the very last class of the entire program Gil stood in front of the class and said:

Here's what we know about adolescents: They get better. If there is an adult in their lives that cares about them as they are going through adolescence, they get better faster and they do less harm to themselves during adolescence. Thank you.

With that, he concluded the class. Those few sentences delivered in less than a minute is what the entirety of my graduate education at Harvard boils down to. Sure, there've been times when I thought that $75,000 was a little too much to pay for that nugget of wisdom, but the fact remains that all of my years of work that followed, all of my research, and all my experiences have done nothing but strengthened the validity of that statement.

I recently asked Gil if he remembered making that statement and what motivated it.

I was referring to a study of kids who were hospitalized in a major psychiatric hospital as young adolescents. When they

70

were followed up over 10 years we found that the majority, even though these were pretty serious (I mean, hospitalization was not something you would do with lots of kids), of the kids were getting better. So what makes them get better? When we interviewed the kids, it often was the childcare worker—the one who was least paid in the system but most directly available, who knew what was doing on in the life of the kid, who the kid called by the first name—rather than the doctor who the kids were describing a lot and reporting as just a really critical figure. That's where this idea came from.

Kids need adults, adults who are not their parents but are adults nonetheless. Kids need adults who act like adults and not like friends. Kids already have friends. They do not need more friends. They need those things that are unique to adults, such as experience and perspective.

Nonparent adults offer kids an opportunity for another model of successful behavior. Nonparent adults also provide kids with an opportunity to explore ideas, feelings, and mistakes with an adult who, like a parent, has a greater understanding of the world but whose role is different than the parent's dual role of protector and teacher.

Gil explains the difference between parent and nonparent adult relationships like this:

> There's a role that gets defined, and it isn't defined by parent–child relationships but is defined by an adult–kid relationship. And I think those are usually a little easier to define because they don't have the same history, like from baby to the present, and they don't have all the sibling issues, and so it is kind of less intense. And I think typically that creates a different dynamic, one that can actually be often more supportive because the kid doesn't have to push against it maybe quite as much, or, if they push against it, the boundaries can be clearer than when the kid pushes against the parent who simultaneously sees an adolescent but remembers when the kid was just three years old.

You may recall from the previous chapter that the opinions of their parents are terribly important to kids. Consequently, they often have a difficult time admitting to what seem to them to be confusing or difficult thoughts or emotions. A kid can share these things with a nonparent adult, and that nonparent adult can offer the same guidance and insight as a parent without the kid worrying about damaging her relationship with her parents.

Relationships between nonparent adults and kids often are referred to as "mentoring relationships" and, when they have been studied, as Gil described earlier, they have been shown to have many benefits.

In a 1995 landmark study from Public/Private Ventures, called Making a Difference, kids in eight different Big Brother/Big Sisters programs were randomly assigned to treatment or control groups. The kids in the treatment group were paired with mentors, while the kids in the control group were placed on a waiting list for the duration of the study. Those kids with mentors fared much better than did their counterparts without mentors. Kids with mentors were less likely to start using drugs, less like to start using alcohol, and less likely to get into fights.

*Social Impact of Mentoring on Kids (5–18) with Mentors
Compared to Kids without Mentors*

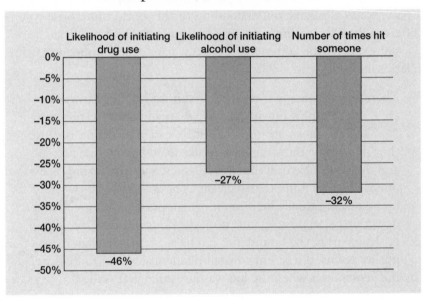

Source: Public/Private Ventures (2000).

As important as the things that kids with mentors did not do are those things that they did do. Kids with mentors, the study found, have better school behaviors and performance.

Academic Impact of Mentoring on Kids (5–18) with Mentors Compared to Kids Without Mentors

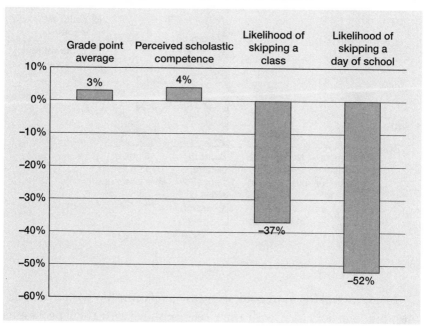

Source: Public/Private Ventures (2000).

Subsequent studies have continued to demonstrate that kids need adults. A 2006 study from the Office of Juvenile Justice and Delinquency Prevention and Public/Private Ventures, called Positive Support, reported that a relationship with a nonparent adult can fundamentally change a kid's outlook. It suggested that kids with mentors are less likely to develop signs of depression. In addition, signs of depression are more likely to disappear from kids who have mentors.

Impact of Mentoring on Depression Among Youth (8–22)

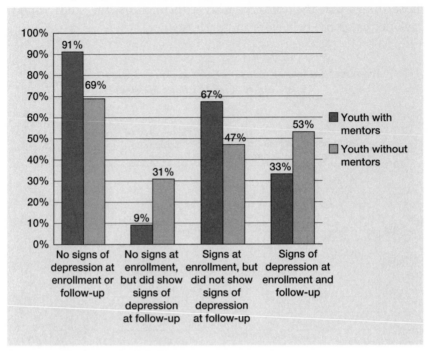

Source: Public/Private Ventures (2000).

In addition, kids need adults because a relationship with a nonparent adult can help kids with their relationships with their peers and with their parents. Regarding friendships with peers, nonparent adults are more mature than kids' peers and less subject to the forces that affect a peer-to-peer relationship. Consequently, kids can practice relationship skills and explore the mechanisms of friendships with a nonparent adult and receive insight into successful human interactions.

Likewise, kids need adults to help them understand their relationships with their parents. A relationship with a nonparent adult can offer a kid insight into that kid's relationship with her parents, providing an explanation for why the parent may be acting and reacting certain ways, and helping the child navigate that very complicated relationship that all humans have with our parents.

That kids need adults to strengthen their other relationships is not theoretical. It is proven. In the same robust study of mentoring cited above, researchers found that kids with mentors had better relationships with their parents and their peers compared to kids without mentors.

Relationship Impact of Mentoring on Kids (5–18) with Mentors
Compared to Kids Without Mentors

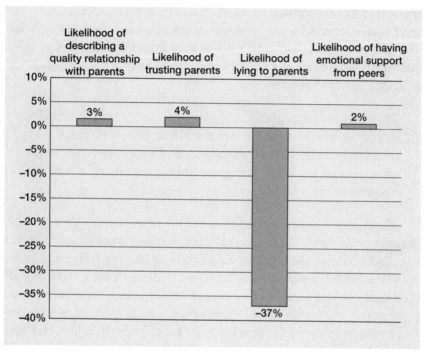

Source: Public/Private Ventures (2000).

In Chapter 4, I mentioned that parents have a dual role as protectors and teachers. I also mentioned that parents need to develop presence, persistence and patience in order to be effective. It turns out that the role of the nonparent adult is very different. In studies of effective mentoring relationships, it appears that a nonparent adult is most effective in helping a kid when that nonparent adult is not directive, not explicitly a teacher. It seems that a nonparent adult is most valuable as a consistent adult who does not put many transactional boundaries on the relationship with the kid. Where parents have to set boundaries and exact rewards and punishments in order to protect and educate their children, nonparent adults, while not condoning or promoting bad behavior, do not dole out punishment. It is a very fine line, but the nonparent adult needs to express allegiance to the child that is unconditional and unwavering, which means that negative behaviors are not condoned but they aren't punished, and positive behaviors are not ignored but they are not explicitly rewarded. Gil described it to me like this:

> That person—if available and knows what the kid is actually doing, knows how to talk to the kid in a non punitive way with being really straight and direct and authoritative in some ways—seems to be a very powerful ingredient of a healthy navigation, even after significant distress.

The role of a nonparent adult in the life of a kid can be a very frustrating one for the adult because the relationship is one sided. The kid talks and acts, the kid asks questions and requires attention and time, but the adult may not get any of that in return. That's okay. We all need relationships that offer mutual affirmation and opportunities for growth, but we adults should expect that from relationships with our peers, not from our relationships with kids. Understanding this and setting this expectation when you help other adults mentor kids will benefit those relationships.

Although the role of a nonparent adult in the life of kid is different from the role of a parent, both require patience, presence and persistence. Once again, this has been proven in some very robust studies and identified in meta-analyses of a great many more mentor programs.

Effective mentors are able to be patient and allow a bond to form between them and the mentee. To be authentic, the bond must form at a natural pace and in an environment that is conducive to friendships. This is why effective mentoring relationships often involve little more than hanging out with a kid, but this is precisely what the kid needs from the adult; the opportunity to enjoy a relationship that is free from the pressures associated with peer or parental relationships.

Effective mentor relationships also are persistent in that the mentor is a stable and regular figure in the life of the mentee. Meetings between the mentor and mentee can be counted on to occur consistently. Obviously, this persistence works hand in hand with patience to help establish trusting bonds between the adult and the kid.

Finally, an effective mentor is present in the life of mentee. Not only do the meetings need to occur consistently, but the meetings need to be sufficiently long as to allow for the mentor and mentee to learn about each other and get comfortable being around each other. Effective mentors also are present over time. We need to acknowledge that if we are going to be an adult in the life of a kid, we need to commit to being present in her life for at least a year. The benefits to the kid only grow the longer that we can be present.

Understanding the Three Ps as They Apply to Mentoring Relationships

Like parents, nonparent adults also need to be patient, present and persistent to make a difference in the life of a kid. However, the three Ps mean something slightly different in the mentoring relationship.

Patience

To make a difference in the life of a kid, the adult must be patient and allow the relationship to develop trust and intimacy naturally.

Persistence

To make a difference in the life of a kid, the adult must be persistent and become a regular fixture in the life of the kid that she can rely on.

Presence

Not only must meetings between the adult and the kid occur with consistency, they must also last. The adult must be present in the life of the kid during each meeting and over time.

6

Kids Need Communities

Back in 2010, John DeBlase was arraigned on charges that he murdered his 3-year-old son and 5-year-old daughter. He and his wife, Heather Leavell-Keaton, already were in custody, having been arrested earlier on child abuse charges.

Among other atrocities, the couple is accused of binding their children with duct tape, stuffing them into suitcases, and leaving them in closets for "about 14 hours" at a time.

What upset me most about the story is that the children had not been seen for months. The abuse they received prior to their murders would have left visible marks on them and deeply affected their behaviors. However, nobody from the neighborhood or the children's school or even the extended family said anything. Rather, the murder and abuse only came to light when, ironically, Heather sought police protection from John because she was afraid that he was about to murder their last remaining child, the one they had together.

Kids need communities. They need communities for many reasons, not the least of which is the fact that the group of adults that constitute any given community should do a better job of looking after the kids in that community than would a single adult. If DeBlase's children were a part of a community, somebody would have protected them from John and Heather.

There is something special about a community that seems to make the community, as a whole, more powerful than the sum of the individuals in that community. Understanding that special quality that communities have is difficult, so I turned to my friend, Dr. Thomas Catlaw. Tom is a university professor whose teaching and research focus on the theoretical foundations of government and society. His book, *Fabricating the People: Politics and Administration in the Biopolitical State*, deconstructs what it means to have a representative government, and his numerous articles critically examine things like public administration and community. He had this to say to me about communities:

> What community, at the end of the day, does is provide a broader setting within which people have a sense that their behavior is going to be regulated in some kind of way, that there is a kind of shared or implicit understanding of what expectations are regarding the way in which people are going to act with one another. I think that's increasingly difficult to have these days. I think that it's something that people pine for and very much want, but it's such an individualistic culture that we're living in that it's very difficult to have a community in that sense, and for people to want to suffer—I mean that not in a bad way—the attachments and the restrictions that come along with being a member of a community. Being a member of a community can make you feel warm and fuzzy but it's also restrictive in some sense.

When I say "community," I'm referring to a group of individuals that interact with each other around an explicit set of shared ideals, beliefs and responsibilities.

Many of us are involved in multiple communities. We have work communities, school communities, neighborhood communities and church communities. Each of these communities might be autonomous, but most likely there are overlapping ideals. The adults we are friends with from the PTA often share many of the same values as the adults we are friends with from our civic groups.

Research shows that participating in communities that have explicit sets of shared ideals, beliefs and responsibilities, and allowing our kids to participate in these communities, has several benefits for them.

For example, when adults turn schools into communities by actively involving parents in decision making, oversight, fundraising, teaching and extracurricular activities, the kids in those schools do better.

- Kids have better grades
- Kids have higher test scores
- Kids have higher graduation rates
- There are fewer incidence of school violence

When we study schools where this had happened, we find that it is the shared value of the community that propels this academic achievement, not the wealth or education of the parents. Kids need communities.

Communities have a similar impact on juvenile crime. Nationwide, neighborhood watches, Weed and Seed programs, and other similar initiatives have reduced juvenile crime in neighborhoods by involving residents in each others' lives, by making residents responsible for one another and for their environments, and by involving residents in the decision making around law enforcement. In short, these initiatives build communities, and the juveniles in the communities are better off. Kids need communities.

In 2003, the Parramore neighborhood in Orlando, Florida, had one of that city's highest crime rates. Rather than attempting to reduce crime by enacting harsher punishments or hiring more police officers, Mayor Buddy Dyer created the Parramore Kidz Zone (PKZ). Modeled after Geoffrey Canada's Harlem Children's Zone in New York City, PKZ reduced crime by beautifying the neighborhood, by creating useable public spaces, and by creating extracurricular activities that bring residents in the neighborhood and their children together in activities that are productive and educational.

PKZ created a community in Parramore that values a safe environment. Residents spent more time with one another, they helped clean up dilapidated buildings and parks, and they started accessing the community and educational services offered at those buildings and parks. They started walking the streets of Parramore, something they have been afraid to do just months earlier.

The results for the kids in this new Parramore were impressive. The overall arrest rate for Parramore was cut in half. More importantly, the juvenile arrest rate in Parramore fell by 81% between 2006 and 2010. Although PKZ was implemented originally to curb the crime in Parramore, the math and reading scores for the kids in that community shot up dramatically. Kids need communities.

Impact of the Parramore Kidz Zone Community
on Juvenile Crime in Parramore

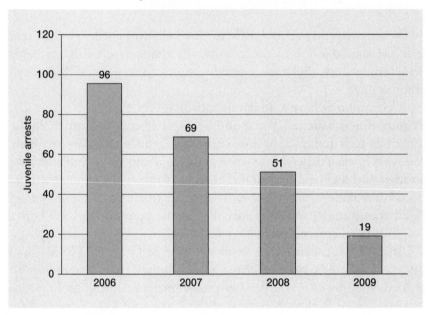

Source: Local Health Council of East Central Florida (2011).

Churches and religious institutions are some of the more obvious examples of communities in the U.S. The shared values of individuals in a congregation often are explicit tenets of that faith. Research shows that kids who regularly participate in a church community are much less likely to abuse substances. Teens who regularly attend religious services are five times less likely to smoke, half as likely to use alcohol, and four times less likely to use marijuana.

Tobacco, Alcohol and Marijuana Use of Teens
(12–17) By Religious Community Involvement

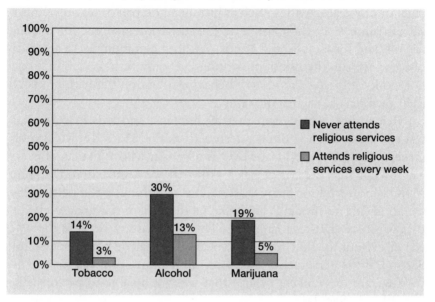

Source: National Center on Addiction and Substance Abuse at Columbia University (2011).

Religious communities also play an important role in kids' decisions to have or not to have sex. In the New Amsterdam Consulting/azTeen Magazine study of teenage females in Arizona, 32% of respondents listed religious reasons as a major influence in their decision. Likewise, 23% listed a religious leader as a person who influences their decision to have or not have sex.

Communities have these effects for many reasons. For one thing, communities act like multiple adults in the life of a kid. When families participate in communities the children from those families don't just have parents or one or two other adults looking out for them, they have all of the adults in the community looking out for them.

As discussed earlier, all humans, and kids in particular, learn from models. Kids look for individuals who have mastered a task that they themselves want to master, they watch how the person accomplishes that task, and then they try to replicate what they just observed. This is true for physical activities, such as hitting a golf ball or playing a musical instrument, but it's also true for social interactions, for making friends, and for establishing bonds. Without communities of adults to observe, we run the risk of presenting kids only with models that may not work for them or models of behaviors that don't fit with or match their own needs, talents, or wants.

Remember, that person that all humans, and kids in particular, want to learn from is often referred to as the More Knowledgeable Other, or MKO. The ideal MKO is a person who is like us in every way except that the MKO has a skill that we want to acquire. This MKO is powerful for many reasons. For one thing, if the person that we are trying to model is a lot like us then there is a greater chance that we share the same language. This is important because then we can talk about the skill in using a vocabulary that we both understand. Second, if the person that we are trying to learn from is a lot like us, then we are more likely believe that we will be able to perform the desired task. She did it, and she is a lot like me, so I can do it, too.

Without communities, opportunities to find and learn from appropriate MKOs are more limited. Consequently, kids without communities are forced to try to learn skills from people who might not be their ideal teachers. As a result, kids without communities are more prone to frustration in learning everything from how to skateboard to how to start and maintain a relationship.

7

Applying the 5 Simple Truths

In this second half of the book, we are going to apply the 5 simple truths to address kids' behaviors as they related to 5 modern issues:

- Television
- Videogames
- Social networks
- Texting
- Bullying

I chose these issues for a couple of reasons. First, they receive a lot of media attention. Second, I get a lot of questions about them from parents.

In approaching each of these issues, we will apply the 5 simple truths in three phases. Although this book will focus on the five issues I mentioned, the approach will work for any issue that concerns you and the kids in your life.

Phases to Applying the 5 Simple Truths

Phase 1: Analyze the perceptions of what the kid is doing

- Remember kids are good
- Look for research that measures the behavior in question

(Continued)

Phases to Applying the 5 Simple Truths (*Continued*)

- Be a parent or be an adult
  - Be a present to the kid to witness the behavior
  - Be persistent in questioning the kid about the behavior
  - Be patient
- Clarify what the kid actually is doing

Phase 2: Analyze the reasons why the kid is doing what the kid doing

- Remember kids are kids
- Decide what developmental purposes the behavior in question serves
- Discern how the behavior is related to the kid's learning preferences
- Draw analogies from your own experience as a kid

Phase 3: Draft a strategy for improving the behavior

- Be a parent
  - Set parameters to protect the kid
  - Create explicit rules that govern the behavior
  - Be persistent in enforcing the rules
- Be an adult
- Model the desired behavior
- Establish communities that reinforce the desired behavior

PHASE 1: ANALYZE THE PERCEPTIONS OF WHAT THE KID IS DOING

Whenever we are troubled by our kids' behavior, either because of something that we have observed or something we read or heard about on television, we need to remember that kids are good. This will keep us from becoming too alarmed and reacting irrationally. Reminding ourselves that our kids are good also will help stop us from treating our kids with suspicion, from making accusations, and from other behaviors that will create barriers between them and us and thwart real communication.

Next, we need to clarify what actually is happening. We can do this by:

- Being present to our kids to observe their behaviors
- Questioning our kids about those behaviors in a way that is persistent but patient
- Look for research that measures the behavior in question

As I've already demonstrated, the actual conclusion of research cited in a news story may be very different from what gets stated in a headline. We need to be savvy consumers of research and rely on large, national studies that are replicated annually. We also can trust research if it is cited by many other researchers and academics. Google Scholar tracks how often academic articles and studies are cited, and the Resources section of this book lists sources of good information about the behaviors discussed in these pages.

PHASE 2: ANALYZE THE REASONS WHY THE KID IS DOING WHAT THE KID DOING

Once we have clarified what our kids actually are doing, we can begin to attempt to understand why they are doing what they are doing. We do this by remembering that kids are kids. As kids, their behaviors are linked to developmental needs and reflect their learning preferences. It is useful for us to review what those developmental needs are and to decide if the behavior is explained by the needs. For example, are they acting out of a need to demonstrate competency? Is their behavior evidence that they are struggling to learn how to have relationships with peers? Are they attempting to discover who they are or want to be?

Likewise, we should attempt to discern if the behavior is related to their learning preferences. For example, are they seeking out environments that let them try new things and fail without consequences? Are they repeating behaviors to gain mastery over some element of their lives? Are they struggling from a lack of a More Knowledgeable Other or because things they are being asked to do are too hard or too easy?

In this phase, it also is useful to remind ourselves that we were kids once, kids with the same core needs and struggles as the kid we are attempting to understand. If we can tap into our own worries and concerns during that period of our lives, it will afford us a different perspective on the kids' behaviors.

PHASE 3: DRAFT A STRATEGY FOR IMPROVING THE BEHAVIOR

Any strategy to improve or change the behavior of a kid necessarily will start with accepting our roles as parents and nonparent adults.

If we are a parent, then we start by establishing parameters to protect the kid from the dangers of their behavior. We do this by setting limits and blocking access to harmful situations, inappropriate content, and dangerous influences. Next, we create rules that govern the behavior. These rules should be:

- Explicit—Write them down!
- Prominent—Hang them on the wall, the refrigerator or another space that is well-trafficked in your house.
- Communicated
- Informed by our kids
- Linked to consequences

The point that rules should be communicated is an important one. It is not enough to set a rule. Our kids need to know what those rules are. My own published research has demonstrated that kids who know the rules are less likely to act out.

Finally, as parents, we need to be present to see that the rules are being followed, and we need to be persistent in enforcing the rules and the consequences of not following them.

As parents and nonparent adults in the life of a kid, our most powerful tool for improving the behavior of a kid—stronger than the strongest lock and more powerful than the cleverest law—is our own behavior. We need to model how we want our kids to behave, and we need to be sufficiently present to them so that they can witness, practice and master our modeled behaviors.

Sometimes this will require us to self-evaluate, to examine our own current practices and past habits to ensure that they are consistent with the behavior we want for the kids in our lives.

In the next five chapters, we will apply these phases to specific issues to demonstrate how they work. The information presented is real and (I hope) interesting to you. However, if the behavior that concerns you for your kid is not addressed here, I believe that it still is useful to read these chapters to see how the 5 simple truths get applied.

8

Kids and Television

Science fiction is rife with stories of computers that become self-aware and begin to act on their own. From HAL 9000 to The Matrix, the consequences of this for us humans are always dire. To me, this raises two questions. First, why don't science fiction writers ever imagine computers doing good things after they learn to think on their own? Isn't there at least a possibility that this would happen? Couldn't artificial intelligence develop and decide to devote its energy to rewarding humanity by inventing calorie-free butter pecan ice cream or to writing one more great movie script for Chevy Chase?

Second, why do we concern ourselves with computers eventually acting on their volition when we talk about television as if it already does? Google "television and children." The results include articles like, "Is Television Harmful for Children?" Why aren't there articles like, "Is Computer Harmful for Children?" It sounds silly, doesn't it? Nonetheless, we talk about television as if it is a living a force.

As somebody who has spent many years studying children and television, I can assure you, television is not a living force. Television is a medium. Some of the content it presents is great. Some of the content it presents is horrible. Recognizing the difference and recognizing what our kids watch on television, why they watch what they watch, and what happens when they watch television will help us craft strategies to allow them to get the most out of television while protecting them from its darker side.

THE PERCEPTIONS

Television Causes Violence

Several studies have linked watching television with violent behavior among children. Many of the studies involve solid methodology and have been replicated in many controlled settings. They typically involve the following:

- Exposing children to a certain amount of violent television for a certain amount of time
- Documenting their behaviors or recording their attitudes about violence after that period of watching television

However, the conclusion that television causes the violent behavior or attitudes about violence is faulty one.

If you sat children in front of an unplugged television for an hour and then recorded their attitudes, the children would not exhibit greater violent tendencies towards anything, except maybe towards you for making them sit in front of a dead TV for an hour.

To be precise, television is not causing violence, violent content is, and I agree with the finding of many of these studies that violent content on television can make viewers—all viewers, not just child viewers—more violence prone. I disagree that it is television's fault. Television is merely a delivery system. Although I have never seen it studied, I would wager any amount of money that reading a violent book would increase the reader's propensity towards violence. How many young men rushed off to take part in the San Fermin Festival in Pamplona after reading Hemingway's *The Sun Also Rises*? There are few things in this world as gory (no pun intended) as the running of the bulls, and yet I am unaware of anyone condemning the book for inciting violence. I have never seen an article entitled, "Is Book Harmful for Children?"

If you look at it on a grand scale, the same is true. The facts refute the perception that television causes violence. Television viewing has increased steadily over the last 30 years. You may recall from chapter 3 that youth violence has decreased over that same period of time. If one were to look only at the correlation between hours of television watched and violent crime, one would see a strong correlation. Does watching television actually prevent violent crime? Probably not. However, it is hard to make the claim that television causes violence when television viewing is skyrocketing while violence among kids is declining.

Juvenile Arrest Rates and Household Television Viewership Over Time

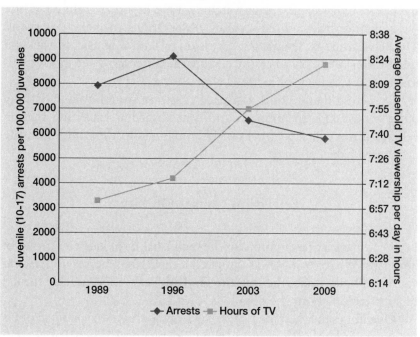

Sources: National Center for Juvenile Justice (2011) and The Nielson Company (2009).

Television Shortens Attention Spans

A recent study demonstrated that watching high-paced animated programs prior to entering a learning environment compromises children's abilities to concentrate. The conclusion is again that television is evil. I will not refute the study's findings. I am going to use them to illustrate exactly what is wrong with some of the perceptions people have about television.

The study, published in *Pediatrics*, found that four-year-olds have a difficult time focusing immediately after watching nine minutes of a fast-paced cartoon.

A different article in the *Sport Journal* described ten years of research showing that fast-paced music helps individuals increase the intensity and duration of physical activity.

An unpublished account of my own wife's behavior indicates that she has trouble sleeping after watching True Blood at night on HBO.

I mention these three separate observations to make this point: The best paintings, sculptures, television programs, music, movies and other forms of mediated reality change the observer. They motivate us to laugh, cry, reflect, or move.

Expecting that a good, fast-paced cartoon would doing anything but motivate kids to jump around is as absurd as expecting that an exhibit of the collected works of Hieronymus Bosch would motivate patrons to bake cupcakes.

Television Causes Obesity

I recently gave a presentation on the media habits of kids to a group of librarians. While the talk was designed to help them better understand younger library users, the question and answer session quickly turned to a discussion about the librarians' own kids.

One librarian asked me, "Why does my son have to spend all of his time watching television and playing videogames? When I was a kid we would all go outside and hang out at the street corner and play."

I thought about my response for a moment. These situations always are difficult. I do not like addressing specific instances. I always would rather speak about general situations. For one thing, I don't want to come across as critical of one person's parenting. Nor do I want to open the door for that person to share or explore feelings are too deep or troubling to address in a lecture setting.

As carefully as I could, I said, "I understand your concern, but let me ask you a question. Do you allow your son to go hang out at the street corner like you did when you were a kid?"

"No," she replied quietly.

Some researchers believe that there is a correlation between hours of television watched and the rise in childhood obesity. Their argument is that all of the hours children spend watching television are hours that should be spent in physical activity. I tend to agree with this logic, but I don't blame television.

Somewhere, somehow in the last 20 to 30 years we began to fear for our kids' safety and stopped letting them play outside in our neighborhoods. We did this in spite of the fact that crime in our communities has been steadily decreasing. Even abduction, the crime we parents fear the most, has been declining. In 1999, the last year for which we have published data from the U.S. Department of Justice, there were 115 "stereotypical" kidnappings (where a stranger or acquaintance takes and kills the child or demands ransom or intends to keep the child permanently) nationwide. Do not get me wrong, a single kidnapping is too many, but according to the National Weather Service a child is about four times more likely to by hit by lightning than to be kidnapped in this manner we fear the most.

So while I agree that children watch too much television, I do not blame television. Rather, I blame our own fear. When children are not allowed to run outside and play in communities, television can be an enticing substitute for actual experience. When too much time is spent with television there is obesity, but, again, I do not blame television.

WHY TELEVISION

Kids watch a lot of TV. A typical kid watches about four and half hours of television a day. A typical household watches more than that. Why? What do kids get from watching television?

Kids like television for many reasons. First, most of the television programs that kids watch take place in their own fantasy universes.

While these fantasy universes can be imaginative, the rules that govern them often are quite simple.

Consider SpongeBob SquarePants. Although Bikini Bottom, the undersea setting of SpongeBob SquarePants, defies the laws of physics and is home to remarkable characters, rules that dictate how SpongeBob and the rest of the cast live and interact are far simpler than the rules of everyday life. The characters are not concerned with macroeconomics, war, or planning for the future. Rather, SpongeBob, his friends, and really the cast of all television programs that kids tend to like, are concerned with what is immediate to them in their environment. They interact with each other without subtext, and when the characters are interacting with each other, they are not preoccupied with work or school or how they are being perceived by others.

Because the rules of these television program worlds are simple, they are easy for kids to comprehend. Every program has a finite number of characters, and kids can learn all of them and demonstrate mastery over the program. In the real world, it is hard just to have mastery over the topics in the evening news. Feeling mastery over the world of a television program helps kids feel in control of their own lives.

In addition to affording kids opportunities to feel mastery over a microcosm of society, the television programs that are most popular with kids model interpersonal relationships. Again, these relationships occur in the controlled setting of the television program, which makes them easy for kids to comprehend.

You may recall from Chapter 2 that kids in the tween and teen years have transitioned away from a world of the home, where the only things that mattered to them were the opinions of primary care givers, to a world where the opinions of peers matter more and more. At the young end of the tween-to-teen continuum, kids must learn what it means to have peers, to live in this world where our peers define us and how we feel about our own worth. As they age through the tween-to-teen continuum, kids begin to ask, "Why am I?" Kids on this end of the continuum look for models of to help define who they are and who they want to be.

At their core, the most popular television programs for kids are all about relationships. They explore what it means to be friends and what it means to encounter difficult situations, conflicts and misunderstandings, and to resolve them. Because these interpersonal relationships are presented in fictitious worlds that are less complex than the real world, kids are free to focus on these interpersonal relationships on a very basic level, but that is precisely where kids want to learn.

Television programs also are potentially important to kids (and maybe to all people) in that television programs remain one of the few things that can create common ground that kids can use to relate to one another.

In Chapter 2, I mentioned that one of the things that has changed about the world of kids is access to media. The sheer amount of media is important, but equally important is the customizability of those media. All of the media that are available to us have made it possible for us to watch, read, and listen to things that we already know that we like. Some sociologists are worried that this customizability will give rise to idiosyncrasy and deteriorate the common ground that kids and all humans need in order to relate to one another.

For example, I'm a big fan of Elvis Costello. If I were so inclined, I could fill my iTunes with nothing but Elvis Costello songs. I could set up an Elvis Costello channel on Pandora. I could go on YouTube and spend all of the time I allot for viewing videos watching Elvis Costello interviews and concerts. Furthermore, I could set up my DVR to only record programs in which Elvis Costello appears. Finally I can spend all my social interactions with the other members of Elvis Costello message boards.

If we use media in the way I describe above, we run the risk of destroying shared experiences. Without shared experiences, we would have less and less in common with each other. There would be less for us to talk about. There would be fewer ways for us to start conversations, and our similes and references would not make sense to one another.

Fortunately, this type of behavior does not seem to be taking hold the way that it could, given the types of media that are available to everybody. Instead, kids generally have a shared experience in television programs. This is not nearly as prevalent as it used to be. For example, 60% of the household in the U.S. watched the last episode of M*A*S*H. You could walk down the street the day following the airing of that TV show and have a better chance than not of being able to discuss the program with somebody you met randomly on the street. Nowadays, less than 8% of the population watches a "hit" TV show.

STRATEGIES

I hope that you now believe me when I say that television is not, in and of itself, the singular force of evil that some make it out to be. Television can be good and can serve a useful role the lives of our kids, and television can be bad. Here are some strategies for helping kids experience the good of television while avoiding the bad.

Television Strategy 1: Use the V-Chip and the TV Rating System

Raise your hand if you own a television that is equipped with the V-Chip.

Now raise your hand if you have a television that was made after January 1, 2000.

If you have a television that was made after January 1, 2000, you have a television with a V-Chip. V-Chips allow you to block or grant access to television programs based on that program's TV rating and other descriptive information that networks assign to each program. By Federal law, all televisions made after January 1, 2000, and sold in the U.S. have this capability.

One strategy for assuring that our kids have the television experience we want them to have is to utilize the V-Chip to block access to television content that we believe is inappropriate.

Let me explain what I mean by inappropriate television content. In Chapter 4, I demonstrated how kids need parents to protect and educate them. Because of their lack of experience, kids do not always know how to interpret what they experience. For example, we know that kids on the younger end of the tween-to-teen continuum do not always recognize sarcasm. Interpreting sarcasm requires experience. Sarcasm also requires cognitive development that many younger kids have not attained. Consequently, adults interpret sarcasm one way, but younger kids might interpret it in a way that is opposite of what was intended.

Another thing that kids need help interpreting is the difference between moral and immoral behavior. With the rise of the antihero in Western literature, television, and movies, consumers of content increasingly are asked to address the issue of what is good and what is evil. This is very interesting to adults. Kids, who have less experience than adults and simply know less, have a harder time interpreting and formulating tenets from morally nuanced behavior.

As an example, consider Robert Ludlum's character, Jason Bourne. Is Jason a good guy? Jason knows how to kill, can kill, and does kill a lot of people in the books and movies, and he is the central figure in the works. What conclusions should kids draw from this? Should they infer that it is morally good or desirable to be somebody who knows how to and does kill a lot of people? There are subtleties like this in many television programs that kids do not have the experience, knowledge or capacity to interpret on their own.

Here are some elements of television programs that I believe kids need help interpreting:

- Violence
- Sex
- Sarcasm
- Parody

By using a V-Chip we parents are assuming our roles as protectors and teachers. We also are connecting our kids to the larger community of television experts and accessing their knowledge about which programs are appropriate for whom and why.

In using the V-Chip, we need to be explicit with our kids about why we are allowing certain content and not allowing other content. We should base these decisions on principles that we can apply across programs. Of course, no set of television rules would be complete without guidelines for how much television can be watched and under what circumstances it can be watched. I also recommend writing these rules down. Having written rules helps enforcement of them seem more objective and reasonable, which leads me into the next strategy.

Television Strategy 2: Write Rules and Limit Television to Communal Spaces

A V-Chip will block programs based on their characteristics, but I never said that kids need blocks. I did say that kids need parents, adults, and communities. I am leery of using blocks, locks, alarms and other devices as substitutes for direct parental or adult supervision.

A V-Chip is an interesting first step in protecting kids from unwanted television content, but it is by no means a panacea. Myriad confusing and ambiguous situations present themselves even in the most seemingly innocuous television programs. One way to help ensure that our kids are watching only those programs that, by their descriptions, have content that is not objectionable to us parents while still providing opportunities for us to help interpret what is in those programs that our kids are allowed to watch is to have televisions only in the community spaces of our homes.

Remember, I'm a defender of television. I like television. I think there's a lot to be learned and gained from the best of television. However, I cannot locate a single piece of research nor can I construct a single argument to support the idea that it is necessary for kids to have televisions in their own rooms so they can watch programs without supervision or parental input. However, I do have research that shows that as televisions move away from communal spaces within the home and into bedrooms, kids are less likely to have or follow rules about what they watch and when they watch it.

Total Time in Hours Youth (8–18) Spend with Media by TV Placement and Existence of Media Rules

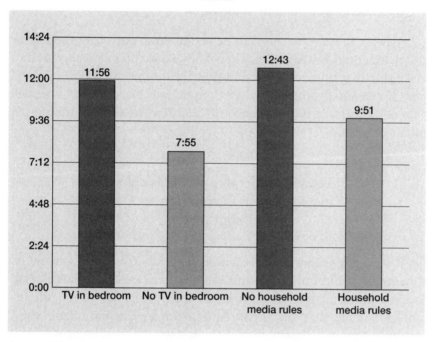

Source: Kaiser Family Foundation (2011).

One of the skills we parents need to develop is presence. It is difficult for us to be present to the television lives of our kids, to protect them from difficult content, and to teach them the lessons inherent in television programs if our kids are watching television alone in their rooms.

In addition to locating the television in a communal room of the house, I recommend crafting rules for television viewing that address the following:

- Under what circumstances television is permitted (e.g., after homework, if grades are satisfactory, if chores are complete, etc.)

- How much television can be watched
- Approved programs or networks
- Consequences of violating these rules

As with all rules, we need to be persistent in enforcing these rules and in exacting consequences when rules are violated. We also need to make sure that our kids know and understand the rules. Writing these rules down and posting them in a conspicuous place in the home will help our kids learn the rules and will help resolve disputes should the rules be violated.

Television Strategy 3: Have Your Kids Apply for Permission to Watch Programs

I believe that television can play a useful role in a kid's development. As I mentioned, television programs can be shared experiences. For a kid to watch the same television programs as her peers can be very important to helping that kid initiate and create sustainable relationships with those peers. Consequently, I think it would be wrong for us parents to decide what programs our kids can watch without input from our kids.

I also think it's wrong for kids to dictate what they watch. That is why I suggest an application process.

If a kid wants to watch a television program and watch that program regularly, have her apply formally for permission to watch the program.

I recommend an application process that involves the following:

- Your kid describes the program, what it is about, and why she wants to watch it.
- Your kid explains where it fits with her other priorities such as homework, sports, Internet use, and playing videogames.
- After reviewing the application, you and your kid sit down together and watch a whole episode of the television program while your kid explains to you what she likes and dislikes, who the characters are, and what motivates the characters.

Who knows? You might even end up liking the programs your kid applies to watch. In addition to creating a shared experience for your kid and her peers, it might end up being a shared experience for your kid and you.

Of course, if your kid is reluctant to apply to watch a given program, this is good evidence that it might contain inappropriate content.

In enacting an application process, we are creating a system to help us be present, patient and persistent in the lives of our kids. Mindful that kids are kids, we can use the applications help us understand how a television program fits how our kids want to learn and who our kids are developmentally. Instead of making snap judgments based on our perceptions of a television program, we are operating under the assumption that our kids are good and using opportunities like this to have meaningful interactions with our kids.

Television Strategy 4: Watch Television With Your Kid

Earlier in the book I alluded to a study I did with parents and their kids that focused on what parents knew about the programs their kids watched on television. I designed a study in which parents and their kids were brought into a research facility and divided into two rooms and two separate focus groups. In one room, I had eight parents sitting around a table. In the room next door, I had their kids—all 10-year-old boys and girls—sitting around a duplicate table. The children sat in the same seat or position at the child table as their parents did at the parent table next door. This way it was easy for me to know which child belonged to which parent as I moved back and forth between the rooms.

I started with the parents and asked them a very simple question. I asked them what their children watch on television. You may recall that the first mother said, "My son watches about one hour of television a night, and he only watches the Discovery Channel." The second mother said, "My son is allowed to watch a half hour a night, but only after his homework is done. He likes the History Channel." And I told you that the third mother said, "My son watches fifteen minutes a night."

I did not tell you about the fourth parent.

The fourth parent, the only father in this group of parents, was visibly anxious. Sheepishly, he said, "My child watches CSI every night."

For those of you don't know, CSI: Crime Scene Investigation is a fairly graphic police drama. It is rated TV 14. Again, his daughter is 10.

He cleared his throat and continued, "We watch it together. We both really like the science of it. We also like to try to figure out who did it."

Then he stopped, possibly because the other parents were burning holes into his skin with their eyes.

I went next door. I asked the first boy—the one whose mother said that he watches an hour of Discovery Channel at night—what he watched on television the previous night. "American Idol," he replied. "After that I watched . . ." and he proceeded to list several more programs.

I asked the same question to the boy whose mother said that watches an half-hour of the History Channel a night. "I watched WWE wrestling." As soon as he said "wrestling," the third boy, the one whose mother said that he watches 15 minutes of television a night, screams, "Did you see the match last night?" He then jumped up onto his chair and began to act out the wrestling match.

I was so shocked that I let it go on a little too long.

After calming the boys down, I asked the fourth child at the table what she watched on television the previous night.

"I only watched one program," she said. "I watched CSI with my dad. We both like science stuff, and we try to be first to figure out who did it."

Despite watching a television program that was rated for viewers much older than her, I believe that girl had the healthiest television life of any of the kids there. Her parent was very aware of what his daughter was watching, and he was even watching with her.

They were discussing the program, and, in doing so, he was helping her interpret what was being said and done. Of all of the parents I mentioned, he was the only one who was present to his kid's television life. For all of the tricks, techniques and rating systems, nothing can take the place of a parent.

9

Kids and Social Networks

R ecently a lot of attention has been given to the fact that many users of social networks, like Facebook, are younger than the prescribed age of 13. Many advocacy groups were outraged. They presented theories of why social networks might be harmful to kids, but few cited any hard evidence. This gave rise to several perceptions regarding kids and social networks.

THE PERCEPTIONS

Kids Get Bullied and Harassed in Social Networks

Kids do harass other kids online. Kids also bully other kids. Whether or not the existence of social networks has increased the total amount of bullying is up for debate. However, there is some evidence to support that it has.

Research into the types of people who engage in bullying indicates that cyberbullies are different than direct, in-person bullies. Unlike direct bullies who bully face to face and rely on their size to control the victim, cyberbullies use their technical expertise to create the imbalance of power that is the defining characteristic of all bullying. Consequently, technology is allowing a new breed of kid to bully.

That being said, it is hard to measure the prevalence of bullying in social networks. Few studies of cyberbullying have adopted a consistent definition of bullying, so we often are left comparing apples and oranges. The School Crime Supplement to the National Crime Victimization Survey is the best source for information on bullying and cyberbullying. Its most recent report indicates that 6% of students ages 12 through 18 were threatened, insulted or made to feel bad by something another student texted, e-mailed, instant messaged, posted online or communicated while playing an online game. Because of how the questions that make up this measure are worded, it is impossible to know how many of these incidents occurred in social networks. It also is impossible to know how many of these acts were intentional and repeated, two things that the definition of bullying requires. Consequently, our best guess for the number of kids who experience cyberbullying in social networks is a number less than 6%. In contrast, 28% of students, ages 12 through 18, had been bullied directly or in person.

Online harassment and sexual solicitation are easier to measure because they don't have the element of intent that is required by the definition of bullying. An article published in *Pediatrics*, the office journal of the American Academy of Pediatrics, found that 9% of respondents, ages 10 to 15, were harassed in social networks, and 4% received unwanted sexual solicitation. The authors' conclusion was: "Broad claims of victimization risk, at least defined as unwanted sexual solicitation or harassment associated with social networking sites do not seem justified."

The New Amsterdam Consulting/azTeen Magazine study of teenage girls in Arizona found that many respondents had experienced harassment online, but the incidence of harassment in social networks, text messages and e-mail is much lower than they experience at school in the mall or at their jobs.

So let's consider this perception partially true. Social networks do offer a new venue for bullying. However, the hysteria around cyberbullying in social networks seems out or proportion when direct, in-person bullying is many times more prevalent.

Social Networks Have Increased the Incidence of Child Abductions

Child abductions that have stemmed from abductors meeting and fostering relationships with kids online are horrifying. Every effort should be made to prevent these incidents and to protect our kids from pedophiles who stalk their prey online.

That being said, there is no evidence to support the notion that incidents of child abductions in the U.S. have increased since the advent of social networks. As discussed in the previous chapter, the only available data on this topic indicate that child abductions were trending in a good direction.

I mention this not to say that we shouldn't be vigilant about our kids' participation in social networks. Much of this chapter presents strategies for doing just that. However, popular media constantly ask us to be afraid for our kids. We, as parents and adults who care about kids, have to decide how and when to deploy resources. We cannot be afraid all of the time. Knowing where the greatest dangers are and where they are not will help us make better, more informed decisions for our families and in how we enact public policy.

WHY SOCIAL NETWORKS

If you're a parent or an adult who is actively involved in the life of a kid, you probably already know this, but it is worth stating: kids do not e-mail. For one thing, they don't have to. The technologies that kids are comfortable using—such as digital photography, video media, and other forms of mediated reality—are far richer forms of communication than plain old, asynchronous e-mail. Kids don't e-mail because they don't have to, because social networks offer them multimodal ways of communicating. And this is why they use social networks.

I spent much of the last several years talking to kids about exactly what they do in social networks. Unlike us adults, who use social networks as a diary or as a record of our lives that links our day-to-day events with our pasts and presents, kids do not have a rich history of acquaintances to keep tabs on. Kids use social networks because they offer many different ways to communicate with peers. For example, if they want to instant message or chat with somebody, social networks like Facebook offer a chat feature. If they want to send a message to multiple people at the same time, they can post to their walls and have it read by all their friends. If they want to communicate more visually, they can post videos or pictures. They even can communicate by playing videogames within social networks.

This last point is particularly important, because the sexes differ in how they prefer to communicate. Males like to communicate with action. Males like to engage in online activities, like videogames, with their friends. During these activities the amount of actual information that is expressed in written dialogue is minimal. The gameplay is the communication. In contrast, females prefer to communicate with words. A social network, like Facebook, allows for many modes of communication in the same Web site, which is why kids do it.

There is another reason why kids, especially those on the older end of the tween-to-teen continuum, like social networks.

I was involved in a study of MySpace when it was at the height of its popularity. At the time, MySpace was pretty much unrestricted. Everyone could see everyone else. This made it easier for researchers to track behaviors. Several researchers reported that a significant percentage of users were under the age of 17 and a significant number of them had multiple profiles in which they claimed to be very different people. This confused many people.

My own interviews with MySpace users about this phenomenona helped clarify this behavior by linking it to the developmental needs of kids. In Chapter 2, I mentioned that the defining characteristic of adolescence is that kids begin to ask the question, "Who am I?" One of the ways that young adolescents figure out who they are is by try different personalities. This is easy to observe if we look at the kids around us or think about your own middle school experiences. In middle school, appearances change rapidly.

Appearances change so quickly during this period because kids literally are trying on different personalities to see which fit them. They do this in the real-life world of middle school, where the stakes are high and the consequences are dire. Remembering that kids are kids and that you, too, were once a kid, think back on how hard it was when you were a young adolescent to change or adapt your persona. Yet, kids still did it.

Online social networks offer kids a chance to engage in this very natural behavior of trying on different personalities, but in a virtual space where the consequences of these actions aren't so grave.

Social networks offer an experience that is closer to what Erik Erikson described as "psychosocial moratorium," which, as I mentioned earlier in the book, is a period when individuals are free to experiment to find an identity. Kids figured this out and used the powerful tools of social networks to see what it is like to be different people, to see if these different people who they are online are successful and, therefore, the people they want to become.

I learned that these teenage MySpace users were not looking to deceive anyone or even to date older (or younger) people. Rather, kids were engaging in behaviors that were very typical for their age but using a new, modern tool to meet a very old developmental need. Kids are kids.

STRATEGIES

Online social networks are safer for kids than they often are perceived to be. Moreover, they offer communication tools that match how kids want to interact with their peers, and they offer environments that seem well suited for working through some developmental issues. However, this does not mean that kids do not need oversight when using social networks. As with television, kids need parents, adults and communities to protect them and teach them how to have successful social network experiences.

Here I am defining "successful social network experiences" as those that allow kids to experiment with personae and develop relationships without incurring harassment, inflicting harm on others or doing lasting damage to their identities.

Sharing Infidelity

If you are like me, you are horrified by how much some young are willing to share online.

Maybe it is because, for people of my generation ("Generation X," born between 1961 and 1981), "sharing" often had a negative connotation. Sharing sexual partners spread HIV/AIDS in the 1980s and 1990s. So did sharing needles. In the 1990s and 2000s, we learned that sharing ideas leads to lawsuits and lost fortunes.

So it is of little surprise that members of my generation, now parents, are terrified by our kids' willingness to share intimate details online. It is now a practice among some older teens to share their online passwords with their boyfriends and girlfriends as a sign of commitment.

Where did we go wrong? Marriage. Marriage is where we went wrong.

To our credit, Generation X (born 1961 to 1981) is committed to better marriages than it experienced as the children of Baby Boomers (born 1943 to 1960). As a result, the divorce rate has dropped almost 30% since the early 1980s. However, it still hovers around 45%.

What does this have to do with privacy and kids sharing their online passwords?

According to a study by the American Academy of Matrimonial Lawyers, the past five years have seen a dramatic rise in the amount of electronic data used as evidence in divorce hearings. Generation X is using private e-mail accounts and social networks to carry out its extramarital affairs.

Kids see the damage to relationships caused by online privacy, and they respond by eliminating the privacy. They share. We adults may fault this logic, but I see something kind of beautiful in choosing romance over privacy.

Social Networks Strategy 1: Write Rules and Limit Internet Access to Communal Spaces

I'm not going to recommend preventing our kids from using social networks. Doing so would make our kids stand out as alien among their peers. Also, if you are a typical adult, you are on a social network yourself. Preventing our kids from using social networks when we do so ourselves would seem hyper hypocritical.

I also do not recommend prohibiting online social networks because I do not want to set you up for failure. If we make social networks taboo, then there is a chance that social networks will become more appealing to the very people we are trying to protect.

Instead, I recommend that you to be a parent, because kids need parents. I recommend that you be an adult, because kids need adults.

As parents and nonparent adults, our best strategy for promoting successful social network behaviors is to be present to the social networking lives of our kids. As parents, we must protect our kids by setting rules and parameters about how, where and under what circumstances social networking can and should occur.

As with the rules for watching television, I recommend committing these social networking policies to writing and keeping them in a conspicuous place where they can be referenced regularly.

At a minimum, the social networking rules should address the following:

- When social networking can occur (e.g., after homework, if grades are satisfactory, if chores are complete, etc.)
- For how long social networking can occur
- Guidelines for adding friends
- Guidelines for language
- Guidelines for sharing images and video
- How to recognize inappropriate interactions
- Steps to take if inappropriate actions occur
- Consequences of violating these rules

Research indicates that it is best to allow our kids Internet access only from computers that are in communal spaces, like kitchens or living rooms. This allows us parents to be present physically to the social networking lives of our kids. We are better able to see what our kids are doing, and our persistence is going to give our kids many opportunities to do the right thing. Not only will our presence prevent our kids from doing something that they probably do not want to do anyway (kids are good), but our persistent presence also gives our kids an excuse that they can use with their peers if needed.

As I mentioned in Chapter 8, researchers have studied the physical location of Internet access in the home and whether physical location was related to having and following established rules for Internet use. Those households that limit Internet access to communal spaces are more likely to have rules about Internet use. They also are more like to have kids that follow those rules. Households where children are allowed Internet access from their bedrooms are less likely to have or follow rules about Internet use.

Social Networks Strategy 2: Be a Part of Your Kids' Social Network

This may seem obvious and many of you probably already do this, but being a part of our kids' social networks is an easy way to be present to them. Like only allowing Internet access from computers in communal spaces of the home, having us parents in their social networks gives our kids a built-in excuse not to engage in inappropriate online behaviors.

Some colleagues of mine believe that kids deserve privacy. I am not disagreeing with this. I believe that kids deserve opportunities for private reflection and for thoughts that are their own. I also believe that kids deserve opportunities to form intimate relationships with their peers. None of this is the job of a social network, which, by definition, is a public forum.

I have studied hundreds of kids as they use social networks. Many times I have witnessed a kid admonish an online friend for cursing in an interaction. When I ask kids about these types of incidents, I am invariably told that they do not want bad language on their profiles because their parents are in their social networks. More importantly, the recipient of the admonishment, the kid who posted the cursing, always apologizes and accepts without complaining or teasing the explanation that bad language needs to be curtailed because parents are in the social network.

Social Networks Strategy 3: Model Appropriate Social Networking Behaviors

If we don't want our kids to be too obsessed with their social networking lives, then the first step we need to take is to make sure that we ourselves are not too obsessed with our social networking lives. If we don't want our kids to misrepresent themselves or to share information that is too personal, then it is up to us to make sure that we are not modeling this behavior. Remember, kids need communities. If the shared values of our social network community include discretion, respect, and propriety, and if the adults in the community are modeling and enforcing those shared values, then the kids in the social network community will have a successful experience.

10

Kids and Texting

W e are in a unique period of history. Previous generations of parents and adults have been confused and even angered by kids' style of dress or the music that they listen to or even the words they used to communicate, but as far as I can tell never before have adults been so outraged by how kids are choosing to communicate.

Text messaging initially confounded us adults. Not only did we not understand how to do it, but we did not understand why anyone would want to send a text message. After all, why not just make a telephone call or send an e-mail? Now that more and more adults are texting, we recognize the value of it. However, we still do not understand kids' complete and utter devotion to it.

It is strange that in the world of genocides, climate change, and economic insecurity, parents often seem to me to be more afraid of texting than any other factor in their kids' lives.

This fear, as fear often does, has led to many perceptions about texting.

THE PERCEPTION

Texting is Destroying Language

In studies of transcripts of text messages, researchers find that text messages generally adhere to standard principles of grammar. This includes punctuation. In fact, 80%–94% of all of the words in all text messages are not abbreviated, according to analysis from multiple text message studies. Far from destroying language, text messaging seems to uphold its rules. In fact, text messaging may be promoting language by creating more written words than have ever been recorded.

When texters do abbreviate words, they are not being rebellious or attempting to create a new, clandestine language that nontexters or adults cannot understand. Rather, researchers believe that abbreviations arise from the medium itself. Texters abbreviate words or phrases that are difficult to type on a telephone. Abbreviations make texting faster, which is important because texting, unlike asynchronous e-mail, is a direct form of interaction and being able to respond quickly keeps the communication process alive.

It is worth noting that famed linguist David Crystal argued in *Txtng: The Gr8 Db8* that the language usage in text messages, which includes abbreviations, symbols and pictures to represent words, is consistent with language usage throughout history, from Egyptian hieroglyphs to Leonardo da Vinci through Lewis Carroll. Apparently, kids have been kids for a very long time.

WHY TEXTING

Kids are kids. As they move through the tween-to-teen continuum, the opinions of their peers become more and more important. Kids begin to worry about what they project to other people. Because they lack the experience of an adult and are still learning who they are and what it means to have relationships, kids on the older end of the tween-to-teen continuum feel compelled to monitor all aspects of interpersonal communication. This can be overwhelming to kids in face-to-face situations. Not only do they have to listen to what the other person is saying to try to discern the meaning of the words as they relate to them and to the relationship (relationships being relatively new to them), but kids also have to monitor what they themselves are saying to make sure that what they are saying is acceptable to the other person and their larger societal roles. They have to consider whether the phrase is acceptable, the opinion expressed is in line with the opinions of their peers and if it is consistent with the persona that they are trying to project.

In face-to-face situations, kids also have to process visual cues in order to decipher the meaning of what is being said. They have to worry about what they are expressing with their own facial expressions, body language and appearance.

Texting allows for direct communication with peers that is somewhat easier for kids to control because they do not have to focus on all of the aspects of communication. They can focus only on the words. Furthermore, when the kid types a word or phrase or question, she can review it and regard it before it is sent. The texter can make changes before it gets communicated to the other person. Like the simple worlds of their favorite television programs, kids feel in control of texting and prefer it to telephone calls or face-to-face communication, where there are fewer opportunities to review what one is saying and projecting.

Of course, a kid's need to monitor and control what she is projecting is not new. Holden Caulfield does it in *The Catcher in the Rye*. Richie Cunningham is doing it when he acts like James Dean to ask out Carol Lipton in an early episode of Happy Days. Kids are kids.

When I was in middle school, if a girl liked a boy, she would ask her friend to write a note to that boy or, more likely, to that boy's friend. The girls often would collaborate over the note to make sure that it was vague and worded correctly to ensure that it contained plenty of loopholes, opportunities to deny or retract the note's real intention. There was nothing casual about this casual note passed in study hall, and the response from the boy and his friend would be crafted with equal care, if not more bravado. Kids are kids, and the study hall note of yore has evolved into an electronic communication, but the purpose that those notes served in establishing and maintaining tricky or uncomfortable interpersonal relationships remains intact.

Sexting

I recently received a list entitled, "50 Sexting Acronyms Every Adult Should Know." There was no citation. No author. Just a list. It was distributed presumably as a warning that sexting, sharing sexually explicit images and videos between mobile devices, is an epidemic among kids, so adults better learn what these kids are saying.

(Continued)

Sexting (*Continued*)

The list is fabulous.

The acronyms are crude, complicated, obvious, inventive, and, I began to expect, not commonly used.

I decided to test a few of the terms.

First, I asked my new research assistant, a recent college graduate, about some of the more innocuous acronyms. She was clueless.

Next, I sent a text to a college freshman that I have mentored for a number of years. Here is that exchange:

Sexting Exchange

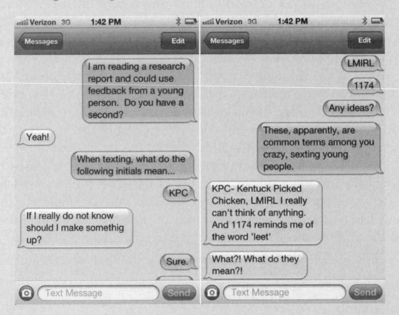

Obviously, the data from my little exercise are anecdotal at best. However, my suspicions are confirmed by a new study in *Pediatrics*, which concluded that sexting is atypical behavior.

For example, the researchers found that only 1% of teens have sent sexually explicit images of themselves from their mobile telephones, which is a stark contrast to the 20% or more reported by some special interest groups.

I was starting to feel smug. My instincts about those "50 Sexting Acronyms Every Adult Should Know" seemed correct. Then I realized, the list is meant to help us adults with our own sexting. You see, it turns out that sexting is more prevalent among adults, 30 to 49 years old, than it is among teens. PTIYPASI.

STRATEGIES

I hope this has shed some light on why kids text, but I do not want to imply that I believe that they should text or that they should text nearly as much as they do. Like you, I'm tired of talking to the crowns of kids' heads as they sit hunched over other mobile devices tapping away. Like you, I am tired of looking across a restaurant at a family that seems to be praying before its meal, only to realize that they are all hunched over, texting. If texting by the kids in your life has gotten out of control, here are some strategies that might help.

Texting Strategy 1: Do Not Give Your Kid a Mobile Telephone

No mobile telephone means no texting.

There, I've solved the problem.

I know this seems impossible. Mobile telephones are such a part of our modern lives, we probably cannot imagine not having one. You probably believe that a mobile telephone is a necessity for your child, but let's examine this for a moment. What would happen if, instead of a mobile telephone, you hand your kid a roll of quarters? There are over 700,000 pay phones in the U.S. If you live in a neighborhood where drug deals were frequent in the 1990s, a pay phone might be less common (and I am sorry); otherwise, there still are pay phones and public phones that can be used in most neighborhoods in most communities.

Parents tell me that their kids have to have mobile telephones for "emergencies." What emergencies? Did you have a mobile telephone when you were 14 years old? What emergencies were you unable to address with the pay phones and public telephones that were available to you?

I added this strategy out of a sense of obligation to the teachers that I work with. Mobile telephones have completely disrupted the educational process. Teachers tell me that telephones interrupt class, cause arguments, and are used to cheat on tests. Depending on the school district, teachers may not be allowed to confiscate or even touch the mobile telephones of the students in their classes, because mobile telephones can be very expensive and schools not want to take responsibility for a teacher confiscating a $500 device. Moreover, teachers tell me that when their students are disciplined for abusing mobile telephones in the classroom, their parents rush to their defense. "More often than not," a teacher recently told me, "when a student is using a mobile phone during class, he or she is texting a parent."

I believe that mobile telephones are very convenient. They revolutionized how I do work, and how I interact with clients. Mobile telephones make it very easy for me to keep in touch with friends and family. But are they necessary for all kids at all times? For example what use do kids have for mobile telephones during the school day? In a supervised environment like a school, what emergency would these kids have to handle on their own and armed only with a mobile telephone?

If we are worried about our kids texting too much, one option is to take away their mobile telephones or limit how and when they use their mobile telephones. It is that simple.

Texting Strategy 2: Use Rules, Locks and Logs

As with television and social networking, it is the job of parents to protect and educate our kids by establishing rules for how, where and when texting is allowed. I also recommend making rules explicit and placing in accessible place where you and your kids and review them as the need arises.

At a minimum, rules about texting should address the following:

- When texting can occur (e.g., before or after school, after homework, if grades are satisfactory, if chores are complete, never between the hours of 10:00 pm and 6:00 am, etc.)
- Circumstances that override standing texting allowance and prohibit texting (e.g., going to a restaurant, being in church, meeting adults, etc.)
- Guidelines for whom can be texted (e.g., friends you know, family members, etc.)
- Guidelines for language
- Guidelines for sharing images and video
- How to recognize inappropriate text exchanges
- Steps to take if inappropriate text exchanges occur
- Consequences of violating these rules

Again, research indicates that kids are apt to follow rules that are explicit and discussed. Research also indicates that knowing the right thing to do in any given circumstance often equates to doing the right thing.

It is increasingly the case that mobile telephone service providers and mobile telephone manufacturers are offering tools that parents can use to help ensure successful texting practices. Depending on the carrier, parents can:

- Limit the number of text messages sent or received
- Block text messages from being sent to or received from certain numbers

- Limit texting by the time of day
- Block inappropriate content from being sent or received
- Prohibit images or video

Carriers are expanding these features regularly. I recommend checking your carrier's Web site to see the features available to you.

Third party providers also offer services that can log all of the texts sent or received by a mobile telephone so they can be reviewed later. Once again, I'm in disagreement with some of my colleagues about the importance of kids having privacy. I do not believe that it is important for kids to have complete control over whom they text message and what they text message. Kids need parents precisely to protect them from saying and doing the wrong sorts of things. If kids had the ability to understand the future consequences of all of their actions, they would not be kids.

Just the same, I believe that knowing whom our kids are texting is more important than knowing what they are texting. To know who our kids' friends are is to be present in the lives of our kids. Logs can help answer that question, but they are not a substitute for persistently and patiently asking our kids about their texting lives.

Texting Strategy 3: Model Appropriate Texting Behavior

Once again, parents and nonparent adults in the lives our kids are their models for appropriate behavior. Kids learn behaviors less from what we say than from what we do. If we want to stop our kids from texting too much or at inappropriate times, we need to examine our own behaviors.

Do we ever interrupt activities with our kids to take or send a text message?

After convincing our kids to run errands with us, do we spend a lot of that time text messaging?

Do we read or send text messages during family meals?

If we text instead of focusing on the kids in our lives, then it is unreasonable to expect our kids to focus on us whenever their focus happens to meet our needs. We must model the behavior we want from kids.

11
Kids and Videogames

Early in 2011, celebrity psychiatrist Carole Lieberman told FoxNews.com, "The increase in rapes can be attributed in large part to the playing out of [sexual] scenes in videogames." Holy crap! Videogames are causing an increase in rape? This is horrible. I feel compelled to take a hatchet to my Wii. Or, rather, I would if this were true.

In fact, forcible rape has been declining steadily for over a decade. Between 2009 and 2010, the year that had just finished when Carole was interviewed, forcible rape declined 5%.

I do not suspect Carole of wanting to intentionally mislead you. As I have discussed earlier in the book, the perception that kids are committing more crimes is pervasive. Unfortunately, these misperceptions lead to even more misperceptions about videogames.

THE PERCEPTIONS

Videogames are Violent and They Make Kids Violent

There is no denying that there are violent videogames, but it is important to recognize that violence is not a necessary characteristic of videogames. In fact, violence is not even a predictor of a videogame's success. Consider the top-selling videogames of all time.

Top-Selling Videogames of All-Time

GAME	PLATFORM	YEAR	UNITS SOLD (IN MILLIONS)
Wii Sports	Wii	2006	79
Super Mario Bros.	NES	1985	40
Mario Kart Wii	Wii	2008	32
Pokemon Red/Green/Blue Version	GameBoy	1996	31
Tetris	GameBoy	1989	30
Wii Sports Resort	Wii	2009	30
Wii Play	Wii	2006	29
Duck Hunt	NES	1984	28
New Super Mario Bros.	Nintendo DS	2006	28
New Super Mario Bros. Wii	Wii	2009	25

Source: VGChartz (2012).

Only one of the top 10 best selling videogames of all time involves shooting. In Duck Hunt, a pixellated hunter and his dog shoot ducks, not people, and the violence is cartoonish. The ducks don't even bleed.

Understanding that violence is not essential to their appeal will become important as we develop strategies for creating successful videogame lives for our kids.

The number of studies linking videogame violence to actual violence is impressive. As with television violence, most of these studies measure kids' behaviors or attitudes about violence immediately after being exposed to videogame violence. As I explained in Chapter 8, the immediate impact of stimuli is undeniable, but these visceral responses do not result in sustained behaviors. When I watch Good Eats, I get hungry, but cooking shows do not create global hunger.

The amount of time kids spend playing videogames has increased dramatically over the last decade. In 1999, the typical 8- to 18-year-old in the U.S. spent just under a half hour each day playing videogames. By 2009, that number had increased almost 500%. In 2009, the typical kid spent close to an hour and a quarter playing videogames in the typical day. If videogames cause violence, then we would expect to see juvenile violence increase as videogame play increases. Instead, juvenile violence decreased over that same period. Remember, kids are good.

Videogames Make Kids Stupid

There is no denying that kids spend a lot of time playing videogames. As I just mentioned, the typical kid spends one hour and thirteen minutes each day playing videogames, which is more time than they spend reading. Because videogames compete for kids' time against things like physical activity, reading, and homework, many people have made the argument that videogames are making kids stupid.

The opposite is true.

Being good at a videogame requires our kids to learn an awful lot. As we will see, the fact that they have to learn is part of the appeal of playing videogames. Unfortunately, it is not always easy to recognize what our kids learn from videogames. The perseverance and problem solving that many videogames teach may not be obvious to outsiders. Furthermore, the knowledge that our kids gain from videogames may not always be valued in traditional scholastic settings.

Is this the fault of videogames? Perhaps. But it doesn't mean that videogames are making our kids stupid. It simply means that what our kids are learning in videogames is not valued in traditional settings.

WHY VIDEOGAMES

The reason that kids find videogames appealing is that videogames match precisely how kids want to learn. Recall from Chapter 2 that for a kid to learn, to acquire a new skill, that new skill must first be attractive or appealing to that kid. There must be something about what that skill does or produces that catches that kid's attention and offers an incentive for acquiring it. In sports, the incentive for learning a better batting stance is more hits and more runs. In school, the incentive for memorizing state capitals is a good grade and accolades from the teacher and parents. In videogames, incentives are levels or points.

Kids acquire skills by observing a model, attempting and failing to do what is modeled, in a place that is relatively free of consequences, repeating the skill until it is mastered, and demonstrating that mastery for validation. This process is very exciting to kids. As James Paul Gee points out in his seminal work, *What Video Games Have to Teach Us About Learning and Literacy*, such environments are rare in scholastic settings, but the environment exists in almost every popular videogame. The few schools that allow for this process have seen amazing academic performance.

Recently, I had the privilege of interviewing a number of poor students at a community college in the Southwest. By "poor students," I do not mean that these individuals have faulty study habits; I mean that they are broke. These were young people who are living below our nation's poverty line and who have come to the realization that an education may be the key to a better life for them.

One young woman confessed to me that her math class has been the single biggest academic obstacle she has faced since returning to school.

She said, "You see, I don't do math."

I laughed politely, assuming that she was making reference to a popular phrase (earlier that day, one of the staff at the college had said to me, "I don't do Starbucks.").

"No," she continued, "I don't do math. I stopped doing math when I was 13."

It caught me off guard. She was serious, and, for a moment, my mind raced as it attempted to comprehend exactly what that meant. I could not imagine going through life without doing any arithmetic.

She went on to describe an incident from her middle school years. It seems that her seventh-grade math teacher had belittled her in front of the whole class for not answering a question about an equation. She had been singled out, derided and made to sit alone at a desk apart from the other students.

What she did or said to deserve such treatment is irrelevant to this point: School was not a safe place for her. It did not afford her the opportunity to try and fail until she got it right. Instead, it singled her out for scrutiny at period in her life, a period in all of our lives, when the opinions of others are incredibly important. As a result, she started associating math with shame and failure, so she stopped doing it.

If she had been inside of a videogame instead of a classroom, she would have been encouraged to attempt the new skill. If she got it wrong, the worst thing that would have happened is that she would have had to go back a few steps or lose one of a multitude of lives. When she eventually gained the new skill, the next level of the videogame would have enforced that learning by forcing her to use that new skill over and over again to advance.

This last idea, that videogames force kids to build on their ever-expanding body of knowledge to succeed, is known as "scaffolding." Scaffolding is a great metaphor. Think about actual scaffolding. If you ask somebody to build the 4th floor of building when they haven't yet constructed the 1st through 3rd floors, that person is destined to fail. You cannot build the 4th floor of a building without the 1st, 2nd, and 3rd floors. But if you ask somebody to build the 1st floor of the building over and over again, that person will get very bored with that task.

Cognitive psychologists tell us that at all learning should scaffold to keep learners engaged, but traditional classroom instruction often does not. Videogames do. This is why kids like videogames. When they play videogames, kids are being kids and are responding to an environment that matches how they are predisposed to learn.

We all have an invisible space around us that separates what we are able to do from what we want to do and could do with just a little more help, and it is a very exciting space. It is known as the "zone of proximal development." The help is the scaffolding that allows us to begin work on the 4th floor after the first three floors are in place. Skills in this zone require all of our previously acquired skills in order to reach them. However, they are not so far away that we can't accomplish them. Videogames are very good at keeping kids in this zone.

Think about a videogame like Super Mario Bros. Finishing a level requires all the skills and moves and tricks that you've got. When you finish a level, you are rewarded with stars and points and . . . a new level! The challenge of the new level is very exciting, and it forces you to build upon you skills such that you begin to wonder why you ever struggled to get through the previous level.

The final reason why kids like videogames is that videogames help meet one of he most basic goals of childhood development. As I mentioned in Chapter 2, one of the primary needs or goals of childhood development is finding pleasure and success. Videogames are very good at providing kids with constant, tangible evidence of success. Videogames do it with scores, coins, points, and levels, all of which are used to reward the player for mastery.

Think about the kids in your own life. Has one of them ever come to you excited that she just completed a certain level in the game or unlocked a certain something-or-other? Did she make you go and look at a meaningless videogame screen? It may be meaningless to us, but it is not meaningless to them. To them it is success, proof that they have mastered a part of the world around them, which is precisely what kids need to do to move across the tween-to-teen continuum.

So we must not dismiss kids when they want to show us their high scores. We must embrace our responsibilities as parent or nonparent adults in the lives of kids. It doesn't have to be meaningful to us. The important thing is that it is meaningful to them.

What's the Deal With Pokémon?

Several years ago, the big mystery among people who care about, study or market to 10-year-olds was Pokémon cards. Why did younger tweens find them so appealing? It's because Pokémon cards fit their brains. As an activity, it was all about sorting and organizing. To be good at the game, a kid needed to demonstrate knowledge of each Pokémon's power and abilities. To younger tweens, another really appealing thing about Pokémon cards is that adults didn't get it. So we, as adults, could not tell them that they were doing it wrong.

STRATEGIES

Just because videogames are good at matching how kids want to learn and help them find pleasure in success, we shouldn't take this to mean that the videogame lives of our kids can go unsupervised. Videogames can have very complicated and even adult messaging, and kids need adults to help them interpret what is happening in videogames. They also need parents to teach them which videogame behaviors are or are not appropriate in the real world. Here are some strategies to help make that happen.

Videogames Strategy 1: Use Videogame Ratings and Parental Controls

Videogames have ratings just like television shows and movies. Created by the Entertainment Software Rating Board (ESRB), these rating recommend a minimum age for unsupervised players and offer descriptions of the content. They are listed on the packages of videogames. We can use them to help gain insight into the content of videogames and to help us determine whether or not a videogame is appropriate for our kids. Like television ratings, ESRB ratings give our kids the benefit of the community of experts that study and review videogames.

In addition, the manufacturers of hand-held videogames and console systems offer parental controls that allow parents to permit or black access to videogames based on their ESRB rating.

As console systems evolve, the parental controls are evolving, too. For example, the Xbox 360 allows parents to specify:

- Which ESRB ratings are allowed
- How many minutes kids can play in a given day or week
- If kids can play against others over the Internet

As you know, I am wary of mechanized control. I do not believe that anything can substitute for direct oversight by a parent or an adult. However, parental controls are a good frontline defense that also can be used to reward desired behavior. For example, we can use the timer in our videogame console system to reward school performance with additional minutes of play.

Videogames Strategy 2: Write Rules and Limit Videogame Access to Communal Spaces

If you have read the other chapters, you know that I am proponent of creating explicit rules to set safe boundaries around the media lives of our kids. Videogames are no exception. Having clear rules and educating our kids about these rules is especially critical to creating successful videogame lives for our kids because videogames, by their nature, sometimes blur boundaries. When a kid is engulfed in gameplay she might not know that her allotted time is up, but interrupting her may prevent her from realizing an achievement at a very critical moment. Therefore, it is important that we have rules that address:

- When videogames can be played (e.g., after homework, if grades are satisfactory, if chores are complete, etc.)

- How long videogame sessions can last
- How kids should respond to parents and adults while they (the kids) are playing (e.g., pause the videogame at the earliest possible moment, turn away from the videogame to answer questions, etc.)
- Lists of appropriate videogame titles
- Consequences of violating these rules

Commit these rules to writing and post them or keep them someplace where they can be referenced regularly. Furthermore, be persistent in enforcing these rules.

As with television and the Internet, I recommend relegating videogames to communal spaces where we parents and other adults can be present to the videogames lives of our kids, monitor what they are doing, and help interpret messages that come from the videogames.

Perhaps more than with the other media, our kids welcome us as audiences to their gameplay. They want us to see them be good at something. They want us to see them achieve.

Videogames Strategy 3: Have Your Kids Apply for Permission to Play a Videogame

As you can tell, my approach to strategies for creating successful videogame lives for our kids is very similar to my approach to creating successful television lives. I like television, and I like videogames. I like that videogames challenge kids and get them excited about learning and acquiring new skills. Videogames also have the potential to help kids connect with their peers, which is why simply dictating which videogames they play might not be the ideal approach.

If your kid wants to purchase a videogame, I recommend having her complete an application in which:

- Your kid describes the videogame, what it is about, and why she wants to play it

- Your kid explains where time for playing the videogame fits within her other priorities such as homework, sports, watching television and using the Internet
- Working from the information in the application, you should investigate the videogame online using Web sites that describe gameplay and offer visuals taken from the videogame
- If possible, rent the videogame and play it with your kid, while you ask questions about the plot, the characters, and the characters' motivation

Playing videogames with a kid is just another opportunity to be present to them. Of course, in accepting our roles as parents or nonparent adults, we need to be mindful of the fact that we play a videogame with a kid to develop a relationship with that kid, not to get a high score. Our own enjoyment of the videogame must take a backseat to patiently and persistently learning about the kid.

This application process has additional benefits. We get gift ideas. It prevents us from being pressured to buy a videogame when we are in a store with our kids. Finally, it gives us an answer besides, "No." And we parents all are sick of saying, "No."

KID: Can I have this videogame?

ADULT: Complete an application and we will see.

KID: But . . .

ADULT: You know the rules.

Videogames Strategy 4: Model Behaviors

If we don't want our kids to become too involved in violent videogames, then we parents and adults need to model that behavior and not play violent videogames in front of them. Likewise, if we do not want our kids to place too much emphasis on videogames, then we cannot emphasize videogames over other activities.

Those of us adults who play videogames need to examine how we behave during gameplay. Do we tune out the rest of the world? Do we get annoyed when we get interrupted? Do we get overly impassioned or use violent language to describe or react to the videogame we are playing? If we answer any of these questions in the affirmative, then it will be difficult to require our kids to behave differently. Kids need parents to teach and protect them, but they are more likely to learn from what we do than from what we say.

12

Kids and Bullying

Much of my recent work has focused on kids and bullying. This is not necessarily by choice. Bullying is a hot topic. The tragic cases of Phoebe Prince and Tyler Clementi made national news and launched bullying into the spotlight.

The abruptness with which bullying entered our consciousness has motivated me to begin all of the bullying trainings I do for educators with a question. I ask for show of hands indicating how many of them have anti-bullying posters up on the walls in their schools or classrooms. I then ask those educators who raised their hands what those new bullying posters replaced. I know that wall space in classrooms and schools is scarce. In a typical school, every square inch of blank wall is covered with learning materials, posters from social campaigns, and flyers announcing upcoming events. I know that those anti-bullying posters had to replace something, so I ask, "Did the anti-bullying poster replace an anti-drug poster? Did it replace a poster on nutrition? Did it replace a poster promoting reading?"

I have been working with and studying kids professionally for a long time. I got my first job in an after-school program in 1988, so I know that bullying is a problem for these kids whom we care about so much. But I also know that it is not a new problem. Moreover, the problems that were in the spotlight last year and the year before, things like childhood obesity and weak academic performance, have not gone away simply because the attention is now on bullying.

141

Bullying is a problem, but it not necessarily the problem that popular media have made it out to be. Our kids are not just bullies and victims. They are sons and daughters, bothers and sisters, athletes and geeks, and preppies and greasers. Understanding this and understanding the real impact of bullying in the lives of our kids will help us craft real solutions, ones that treat our kids as the complete people that they are without overemphasizing bullying in their lives.

The amount of focus that is being placed on bullying in our society has yielded many perceptions.

THE PERCEPTIONS

Bullying Is Getting Worse

Bullying is not a new phenomenon. The Western canon is rife with fictional depictions of bullying that date back centuries. You may recall that Oliver Twist delivered his famous line, "Please, sir, I want some more," after he and his companions were threatened by another boy who was "tall for his age." Remember Piggy from *Lord of the Flies?* Well, the fact that he was called "Piggy" was an act of bullying.

Bullying certainly is not unique to the United States. A World Health Organization study ranked the U.S. in the middle of surveyed countries in terms of bullying prevalence among tweens and adolescents. Which countries are the worst? Well, it turns out that Cole Porter was right: Lithuanians and Letts do it.

But bullying is not getting worse.

The best research indicates that approximately 28% of kids ages 12 to 18 have experienced some sort of bullying behavior in the past year. Measures of the consequences of bullying that we are most worried about—such as suicides, being in a physical fight at school, carrying a weapon to school, or missing school out of fear for one's safety—are all declining. Despite the insistence of the popular media that bullying is an epidemic, our schools safer today than they were 5 years ago, 10 years ago, or 15 years ago. Kids are good, and they increasingly are behaving that way towards each other.

Percent of High School Students Who Carried a Weapon to School in the Month Prior to the Survey

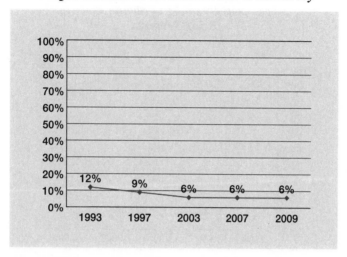

Source: Centers for Disease Control and Prevention (2011).

Percent of High School Students Who Did Not Go to School Because They Felt Unsafe at School or on Their Way to or From School on At Least 1 Day in the Month Prior to Being Surveyed

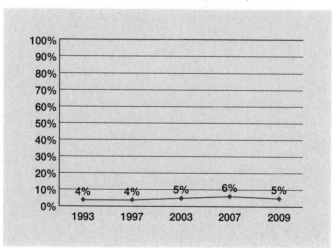

Source: Centers for Disease Control and Prevention (2011).

Percent of High School Students Who Were Threatened or Injured With a Weapon on School Property in the 12 Months Prior to Being Surveyed

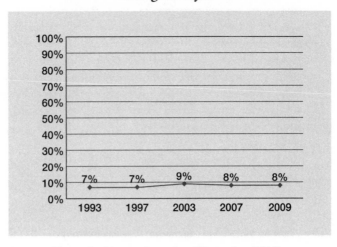

Source: Centers for Disease Control and Prevention (2011).

Percent of High School Students Who Were in a Physical Fight on School Property in the 12 Months Prior to the Survey

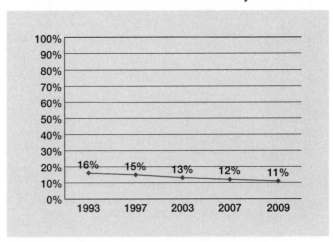

Source: Centers for Disease Control and Prevention (2011).

I know that this contradicts stories that you've read in the newspaper or seen on television. Two factors contribute to the variability in the bullying data: instrumentation bias and testing bias.

Instrumentation bias occurs when two or more different scales, calipers, tools or questions are used to measure the same thing. The bullying studies that are making headlines are not large national studies that have been replicated over time. They are small studies of individual schools or communities, and their definitions of bullying vary wildly and are often quite confusing. Consequently, it is impossible to compare findings across them.

The second reason that bullying seems to be getting worse is the so-called Hawthorne effect. In research, this is known as "testing bias." Testing bias occurs when we change something by the act of looking for it. Bullying may appear to be getting worse, but that is

Suicide Rate for Youth (15–19) Per
100,000 Youth in the Population

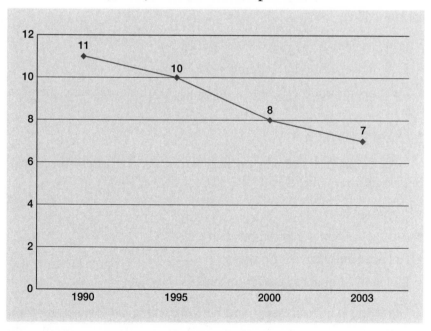

Source: Centers for Disease Control and Prevention (2005).

because we are looking for it so intently. As I explained earlier, when we stop looking for bullying by name and concentrate on the more easily verifiable outcomes of bullying, we find evidence that bullying is on the decline.

Bullying Is a Part of Growing Up and Will Resolve on Its Own

None of the other modern issues I address in this book have perceptions that diverge as much as bullying. People think either that bullying is destroying the fabric of our society or that bullying is a rite of passage.

While it is true that bullying has been around for as long as there is a written history, there is no evidence to suggest that bullying adds value to the human experience. As we have seen, kids who are bullied sometimes react very violently. In very rare cases, victims of bullying have killed others and themselves. More typically, kids who are bullied are more likely to:

- Lose interest in their favorite activities
- Experience a drop in academic performance
- Develop amorphous health complaints, like headaches and stomach aches
- Develop depression

The impact of bullying on bullies can be even more profound. Bullies are more likely to:

- Abuse substances
- Engage in delinquent behaviors
- Fail academically
- Be involved in abusive relationships as they age

Bullying is not necessary, and bullying will not resolve on its own. As with so many other things in their lives, kids need parents and adults to protect them, to educate them, and to model successful ways to establish and maintain relationships.

WHY BULLYING

Before we address why bullying occurs, it is important to understand what bullying is. As I've mentioned, too many things are being described as bullying that actually do not fit the bullying definition. All experts agree that bullying is defined by three characteristics:

- Imbalance of power
- Repetition
- Intent to harm or change the victim against the victim's will

Bullying exists when there is an imbalance of power between the bully and victim. This imbalance of power can take on many forms, but it typically involves a physically larger kid targeting a smaller victim. The bully uses this imbalance of power to repeatedly harm the victim and make the victim do things she otherwise would not do, such as eat alone in the lunchroom, avoid the playground, and surrender possessions. Both threats and actual assaults can result in changes in the victim's behavior.

The imbalance of power is important to distinguish bullying from peer conflicts. Not all kids will get along. If two friends or former friends have a disagreement, it is not bullying because there is no imbalance of power. The kids are equals.

Repetition is important in distinguishing bullying from assault or more minor misbehaviors. If a kid harms a physically smaller kid, that is horrible. It also requires intervention and should be treated as serious misconduct, but without repetition or the threat of repetition it is not bullying. Different dynamics are at play and, therefore, it requires a different response than does bullying.

Finally, using an imbalance of power repeatedly in a way that causes the victim to change her behavior is harassment, not bullying, if the perpetrator did not intend harm. Bullies intend harm and, when confronted, they will blame the victim. Kids who harass are unaware that their actions are causing harm and are apologetic when confronted.

Now that we understand what bullying is and what it is not, let's look at why it occurs. Bullies, it turns out, spend a lot of time alone at home and in their neighborhoods. They seem to lack meaningful relationships with parents, nonparent adults and peers. Furthermore, they often are invisible to what should be their communities.

What bullies believe about themselves or want to project about themselves to their peers or to the larger would-be community often is inflated or out of sync with reality and their actual qualities and abilities. When the disconnect between what a bully wants to project about herself and reality is made apparent, that creates shame in the bully. In addition to spending more time alone, bullies also are more shame prone than typical kids.

Shame is hard for all people to live with, and it is particularly hard for shame-prone bullies. To discharge their shame, bullies inflict harm on other people, often choosing as victims people they perceive to demonstrate or embody that thing that they themselves feel shame about.

Bullies are very good at picking victims. They tend to pick victims who also are invisible to their would-be communities, victims who are not a part of a larger peer group (i.e., who do not have friends) and who do not have the resources that they need to reach out and stop bullying from happening. Bullies also are good at choosing and acting in spots that are invisible to adults.

Much of what I have described here is called "traditional" or "direct" bullying, but many of these dynamics also exist in cyberbullying and indirect bullying. In indirect bullying, the imbalance of power is derived from the bullies' influence on other kids or status within the school. In cyberbullying, the bully uses access to technology or technical expertise to create an imbalance of power. However, the intent of each of these forms of bullying is the same as direct bullying: harm the victim and make her act against her will.

With cyberbullying, if a would-be bully posts something inflammatory about a potential victim, and the victim does not react or nobody sees the post, then bullying has not occurred. Bullying occurs when the inflammatory post causes the victim to be ridiculed at school and shunned or excluded from activities.

STRATEGIES

In the past, anti-bullying strategies either focused on punishing the bullies or mediating. Neither worked.

Harsh punishments for bullies, the kinds promoted by some "zero tolerance" and "three strike" programs, alienated bystanders, who would not report bullying because they thought the punishments were too severe. Likewise, punishing the bully did nothing to prevent future bullying and did not to help any one particular bully develop tools for establishing more successful peer relationships.

Mediation didn't work either. By definition, when two parties enter into mediation, each must make some concessions in order to arrive at common ground. In bullying relationships, the victims have nothing to concede because they did nothing to deserve the bullying. However, a profound side effect of being bullied is that victims often are left believing that they did deserve it. Mediation programs actually were exacerbating this.

What follows are two broad strategies. The first is for preventing bullying in communities. The second is for helping an individual kid who is being victimized.

Anti-Bullying Strategy 1: Create Communities That Do Not Allow Bullying

The effective strategy to stop bullying is to create communities that do not allow bullying. If this seems overly simplistic, it's not.

We adults often are unaware that bullying is occurring. Remember, bullies and victims often are invisible to the adults in their lives. Bullies target victims precisely because they are invisible. Moreover, bullies intentionally choose to act in locations that are not seen by adults.

However, bullying is not invisible to other kids. Young bystanders witness these bullying events. We can prevent bullying simply by including these bystanders in communities that have as one of their explicit and shared values the belief that witnesses of bullying acts must intervene by:

• Quickly finding an adult member of the community

• Supporting the victim

• Banding together with other bystanders to tell the bully to stop

Outside of acute bullying situations, the community can advance its anti-bullying efforts by involving victims and bullies in friendly activities. This makes both victims and bullies more visible to adults and kids in the community. It also gives victims and potential victims friends and resources they can access if a bullying threat ever were to loom again. And all of this serves to model successful relationships to both bullies and victims, something both have struggled to achieve. Kids need communities.

Why aren't bystanders intervening on their own?

I've been fortunate enough to be involved in a few projects that afforded me opportunities to interact with kids directly about their bullying experiences. In one project, I got to interview 10-year-olds about bullying in their environments. These young interviewees were recruited using a set of questions that I hoped would exclude both bullies and victims from the study. I wanted to talk to bystanders. When I did, several interesting things emerged. First, I learned that bystanders generally were unafraid of bullies because they have friends and relationships with adults in their communities, both things make them less-than-ideal targets for bullies.

Despite not being afraid of bullies, few had intervened on behalf of a victim. When I asked why that was, these bystanders told me something equally surprising: They didn't know they were supposed to, and they didn't know what to do to intervene. Nobody had told them.

Kids need parents, adults and communities. They need parents and adults to establish rules and expectations that protect them, and they need communities with shared values to enforce those values through modeling and monitoring of community members. With these things in place, bullying can be prevented.

When we create these communities that intervene and prevent bullying, we need to recognize and reward bystanders for their involvement. Looking out for other members of the community is a sacrifice. Intervening is a sacrifice. While bullies, potential bullies, victims, and potential victims all gain a lot from these communities, bystanders are giving something up.

Anti-Bullying Strategy 2: Model, Model, Model

To prevent bullying, we need to create communities that do not allow it. However, as parents of or a nonparent adult in the life of a kid who is being bullied, there still are things that we can do right now to help the victim.

First and foremost, we need to assure the victim that it is not her fault. Nothing justifies bullying. Bullying is not about the victim. It is about something that is happening within the bully. The victim has done nothing to deserve the bullying, even though the victim often is made to feel as though she has.

Second, we need to assure the victim that it is not her fault. Once this is completely engrained in the mind of the victim, we can move on and help the victim cope with the situation.

I recommend asking the victim what she thinks should be done to stop the bullying. Our kids are pretty impressive. They often know what they want to do to stop the situation, but they need our help as parents and adults to do it.

After we get the victim's suggestions, we need to work with her to refine an approach. Fighting back physically against direct bullying is not an acceptable strategy, despite what movies have taught us. Ralphie's triumph over Scut Farkus, the yellow-eyed bully in *A Christmas Story*, was lucky ... and fictional. In reality, victims often get hurt worse when they attempt to fight bullies. In fact, fighting back often feeds the bully's need to illicit a reaction from the victim while providing the bully with an added incentive to inflict more harm on the victim.

We need to help the victim create a strategy that includes involving adults and appealing to bystanders. If a bully must be addressed directly, I recommend calm assertiveness, saying something like, "I am not going to fight back, but you are not going to bully me any more." Such assertiveness might communicate that the bully is no longer dealing with an invisible victim with no resources or recourse.

The desire for social interaction seems innate in humans, but the ability to do so most definitely is not. How to talk to other individuals, especially around a difficult topic like bullying, needs to be learned. I recommend helping the victim rehearse what she wants to do and say to stop or prevent the bullying. In doing so, we must be sure to address the following:

- What is she going to say to teachers or other adult in the community about the bullying?
- What is she going to say to bystanders to involve them?
- What is she going to say to the bully?

It will take an incredible amount of patience and persistence on our parts, but I recommend that we role-play these scenarios with our kids to model success. Role-play that we are the bully and they are themselves. Then reverse it. Role-play that we are a teacher and they are themselves. Then reverse it. Role-play that we are bystanders. Then reverse it.

With repetition and trial and error, we can work with our kids to develop reactions to bullying situations that are appropriate for our individual kids in their unique situations.

After the acute bullying situation has resolved, we parents and adults can help past and future victims further by helping them be less invisible, and by helping them learn how to have successful relationships. We know that victims of bullying, like the bullies themselves, spend a lot of time alone. We need to teach these kids how to make and maintain friendships. Help the victims in your life understand what they can bring to a friendship. Model social interactions and allow them to rehearse how they would go about making friends. Role-play. If these kids find friends and become members of peer groups, then they cease to be invisible to the community, and they cease to be ideal targets for bullies. Remember, we are not blaming these kids for being victimized. They did nothing to deserve the bullying. Rather, we are helping them form relationships that they want anyway.

I believe that similar techniques can be used with bullies to stop the bullying. We know that bullies feel disconnected from their peers, they don't have communities, and they spend a lot of time alone.

I believe that bullies who can learn to have healthy relationships with their peers will not need to harm others.

If you are the parent of or the adult in the life of a bully, ask her what she thinks she could do to stop the bullying behavior. Explore with the bully how she interacts with her friends. Explain what it means to be in a relationship with another person. Help the bully develop more successful interpersonal skills by modeling those skills and engaging in role play. Bullies, like victims, need parents, adults and communities.

13
Conclusion

K nowing the 5 simple truths of raising kids has changed me, but not just in my role as a father. I see the world differently.

Where some people see problems, I see kids being kids. Where some people see miscreants, I see good kids who are treating each with care and respect.

The converse of this is how upset I can become when I see individuals refusing to be parents or nonparent adults in the lives of kids, or when I see communities adopt values that hurt kids rather than help them.

Two examples of this leap to mind. This first is a little frivolous.

Back in 2010, San Francisco's Board of Supervisors joined Santa Clara County in prohibiting toy prizes from being included in high-calorie, high-fat children's meals.

As you know, I am very concerned about childhood obesity. The prevalence of obesity among 6- to 11-year-olds has tripled in the last 30 years, and it is not going down. Moreover, childhood obesity is associated with devastating health problems (e.g., heart disease, diabetes, etc.) and crippling social problems (e.g., low self-esteem, drug use, bullying, etc.).

However, legislating access to Happy Meals struck me as absurd. Kids already have devices for resisting the potentially hypnotic appeal of burgers and fries packaged with toys. These devices are more commonly known as parents. If we do not want our kids eating high-calorie, high-fat children's meals, then we parents should not buy them.

Furthermore, laws are not substitutes for the presence of caring adults. When it comes to engendering healthy living habits in kids, we already know what works: having parents with healthy living habits.

That tax dollars and legislative time were spent so that adults could shirk parental responsibility angered me, but not as much as my second example.

From 2003 to 2008, a judge in Pennsylvania named Mark Ciavarella received $1 million in payments from the builder of two juvenile lockups for keeping those facilities full. In doing so, the Pennsylvania Supreme Court determined that Mark violated the constitutional rights of about 4,000 kids by denying them the right to legal counsel and the right to intelligently enter a plea. Kids without resources were particularly susceptible to his judicial abuse.

Mark was sentenced to 28 years in federal prison, but the harm he caused the kids he sentenced will linger indefinitely.

This case infuriated me. Why did it take so long for justice to be served? Where were the parents, adults, and communities that were supposed to be protecting these kids?

Knowing the 5 simple truths of raising kids—that kids are kids, that kids are good, that kids need parents, that kids need adults, and that kids need communities—offers solutions to many of the real and perceived problems facing our kids, but these 5 simple truths also create responsibilities. It is hard to look at the facts and not conclude that we adults have a tremendous amount of power in the lives of our own kids and the kids in our larger communities.

What is particularly daunting is the fact that our power lies not in what we say, but in what we do.

I encourage you to take on the challenge head first. Please consider me a part of your community and somebody you can rely on to help you be an adult in the life of a kid. And if it ever seems too daunting, just remember that you already are doing a great job. After all, kids are good.

Resources

American Psychological Association
750 First Street NE, Washington, DC 20002
T: 800-374-2721
www.apa.org

The Annie E. Casey Foundation
701 St. Paul Street, Baltimore, MD 21202
T: 410-547-6600
F: 410-547-6624
www.aecf.org

Centers for Disease Control and Prevention
1600 Clifton Road, Atlanta, GA 30333
T: 800-CDC-INFO (800-232-4636)
www.cdc.gov

Child and Adolescent Health Measurement Initiative
Oregon Health & Science University
707 SW Gaines Road, Portland, OR 97239
T: 503-494-1930
www.childhealthdata.org

Child Exploitation and Online Protection Centre
33 Vauxhall Bridge Road, London SW1V 2WG
T: +44 (0) 870 000 3344
www.ceop.police.uk

Child Welfare Information Gateway
1250 Maryland Avenue SW, Washington, DC 20024
T: 800-394-3366
www.childwelfare.gov

Children's Defense Fund
25 E Street NW, Washington, DC 20001
T: 800-CDF-1200 (800-233-1200)
www.childrensdefense.org

Corporation for National and Community Service
1201 New York Avenue NW, Washington, DC 20525
T: 202-606-5000
www.nationalservice.gov

Department of Education
Department of Education Building
400 Maryland Avenue SW, Washington, DC 20202
T: 1-800-USA-LEARN (1-800-872-5327)
www.ed.gov

Department of Health and Human Services
200 Independence Avenue SW, Washington, DC 20201
T: 1-877-696-6775
www.hhs.gov

KidsHealth
www.kidshealth.org

National Center for Missing & Exploited Children
699 Prince Street, Alexandria, VA 22314
24-hour Hotline: 1-800-THE-LOST (1-800-843-5678)
T: 703-224-2150
F: 703-224-2122
www.missingkids.com

National Center on Addiction and Substance Abuse at Columbia
    University
633 Third Avenue, 19th Floor, New York, NY 10017-6706
T: 212-841-5200
www.casacolumbia.org

National Criminal Justice Reference Service
P.O. Box 6000, Rockville, MD 20849
T: 800-851-3420
F: 301-519-5212
www.ncjrs.gov

National Institute of Mental Health
6001 Executive Blvd., Rockville, MD 20852
www.nimh.nih.gov

National Sherriff's Association
1450 Duke Street, Alexandria, VA 22314
T: 800-424-7827
F: 703-838-5349
www.sheriffs.org

Office of Juvenile Justice and Delinquency Prevention
810 Seventh Street NW, Washington, DC 20531
T: 202-307-5911
www.ojjdp.gov

The Substance Abuse and Mental Health Services Administration
SAMHSA's Health Information Network
P.O. Box 2345, Rockville, MD 20847
T: 1-877-SAMHSA-7 (1-877-726-4727)
F: 240-221-4292

Select References

Agostinelli, Gina, Janice M. Brown, and William R. Miller. 1995. "Effects of Normative Feedback on Consumption Among Heavy Drinking College Students." *Journal of Drug Education* 25 (1): 31–40.

Alfonso, Jacqueline, Thomas Hall, and Michael Dunn. 2012. "Feedback-Based Alcohol Interventions for Mandated Students: An Effectiveness Study of Three Modalities." *Clinical Psychology and Psychotherapy.* doi:10.1002/cpp.1786.

American Academy of Child and Adolescent Psychiatry. March 2011. "Children and TV Violence." *Facts for Families* (13).

American Psychological Association. 2012. "Changing Diet and Exercise for Kids." *Children.* Accessed March 26, 2012. www.apa.org/topics/children.

The Annie E. Casey Foundation. 2011. *2011 Kids Count Data Book.* KIDS COUNT Data Center. www.datacenter.kidscount.org.

Assistant Secretary for Planning and Evaluation. 2012. *"Childhood Obesity.* U.S. Department of Health and Human Services. Accessed March 22, 2012. www.aspe.hhs.gov.

AT&T. 2012. *AT&T Smart Controls.* Accessed March 29, 2012. www.att.net/smartcontrols-SmartLimitsForWireless.

Bauldry, Shawn. June 2006. *Positive Support: Mentoring and Depression Among High-Risk Youth.* (Cornell University) Public/Private Ventures.

Brandon, John. 2011. "Is Bulletstorm the Worst Video Game in the World?" *FOX News.com.* Last Modified February 8, 2011. www.foxnews.com.

Bureau of Consumer Protection. 2012. "CP-Children's Online Privacy." Accessed March 29, 2012. http://business.ftc.gov/controller/cp-children%E2%80%99s-online-privacy.

Calvert, Sandra L., Brian A. Mahler, Sean M. Zehnder, Abby Jenkins, and Mickey S. Lee. 2003. "Gender Differences in Preadolescent Children's Online Interactions: Symbolic Modes of Self-Presentation and Self-Expression." *Applied Developmental Psychology* 24: 627–644. doi:10.1016/j.appdev.2003.09.001.

Centers for Disease Control and Prevention. 2012. "BMI Table for Children and Adolescents." Other Growth Chart Resources. Accessed March 23, 2012. www.cdc.gov/nccdphp/dnpao/growthcharts/resources.

Centers for Disease Control and Prevention. 2012. *2 to 20 years: Boys Stature-For-Age and Weight-For-Age Percentiles.* Clinical Growth Charts. National Center for Health Statistics. Accessed March 23, 2012. www .cdc.gov/growthcharts/clinical_charts.htm.

Centers for Disease Control and Prevention. August 27, 2010. "Births, Marriages, Divorces, and Deaths: Provisional Data for 2009." *National Vital Statistics Report* 58 (25).

Centers for Disease Control and Prevention. December 17, 2003. "Focus Area 18: Mental Health and Mental Disorders: Progress Review." Presentation.

Centers for Disease Control and Prevention. 2012. "Selected Health Risk Behaviors and Health Outcomes by Sex National YRBS: 2009." *Youth Risk Behavior Survey.* Accessed March 21, 2012. www.cdc.gov/healthyyouth/ yrbs/index.htm.

Centers for Disease Control and Prevention. 2012. "Suicide." Facts at a Glace (Summer 2011). Accessed January 27, 2012. http://www.cdc .gov/ViolencePrevention/pdf/Suicide_DataSheet-a.pdf

Centers for Disease Control and Prevention. 2012. "Trends in the Prevalence of Marijuana, Cocaine, and Other Illegal Drug Use National YRBS: 1991–2009." *Youth Risk Behavior Survey.* Accessed March 21, 2012. www.cdc.gov/healthyyouth/yrbs/index.htm.

Centers for Disease Control and Prevention. 2012. "Trends in the Prevalence of Obesity, Dietary Behaviors, and Weight Control Practices National YRBS: 1991–2009." *Youth Risk Behavior Survey.* Accessed March 23, 2012. www.cdc.gov/healthyyouth/yrbs/index.htm.

Centers for Disease Control and Prevention. 2012. "Trends in the Prevalence of Sexual Behaviors National YRBS: 1991–2009." *Youth Risk Behavior Survey.* Accessed March 21, 2012. www.cdc.gov/healthyyouth/yrbs/ index.htm.

Centers for Disease Control and Prevention. June 4, 2010. "Youth Risk Behavior Surveillance—United States, 2009." *Surveillance Summaries* 59 (SS-5).

Chandra, Anjani, William D. Mosher, Casey Copen, and Catlainn Sionean. March 3, 2011. "Sexual Behavior, Sexual Attraction, and Sexual Identity in the United States: Data from the 2006–2008 National Survey of Family Growth." *National Health Statistics Report* (National Center for Health Statistics) (36).

Child Exploitation and Online Protection Centre. 2012. "Scoping Report on Missing and Abducted Children 2011." Accessed March 26, 2012. http://ceop.police.uk/Documents/ceopdocs/Missing_scopingreport_2011.pdf

Child Welfare Information Gateway. 2012. "Parental Drug Use as Child Abuse: Summary of State Laws." Accessed March 23, 2012. www.childwelfare.gov/systemwide/laws_policies/statutes/drugexposed.cfm.

Children's Defense Fund. 2011. "Children in the United States." Last Modified January 2011. www.childrensdefense.org/child-research-data-publications/data/state-data-repository/cits/2011/children-in-the-states-2011-united-states.pdf

City of Orlando. 2012. "Parramore Kidz Zone." Families, Parks and Recreation, Mayor's Children and Education Initiative. Accessed March 26, 2012. www.cityoforlando.net/fpr/html/Children/pkz.htm

Connect with Kids. 2005. "The Big Hurt." DVD. www.connectwithkids.com/educators/products/thebighurt.shtml.

Corporation for National and Community Service. May 2007. *AmeriCorps: Changing Lives, Changing America*. Office of Research and Policy Development Authors.

Corporation for National and Community Service. 2012. "Executive Summary: Volunteers Mentoring Youth: Implications for Closing the Mentoring Gap." Accessed March 28, 2012. www.nationalservice.gov/about/role_impact/performance_research.asp.

Corporation for National and Community Service. 2012. "Volunteering in America 2011 Research Highlights." Accessed March 22, 2012. www.volunteeringinamerica.gov.

DeVoe, Jill Fleury, and Lynn Bauer. November 2011. "Student Victimization in U.S. Schools: Results From the 2009 School Crime Supplement to the National Crime Victimization Survey." Washington, DC: U.S. Department of Education, National Center for Education Statistics, U.S. Government Printing Office.

Disabled World. 2012. "Average Height to Weight Chart—Babies to Teenagers." *Child Disability and Health* (Disabled World). Accessed March 22, 2012. www.disabled-world.com.

Dunworth, Terence, and Gregory Mills. June 1999. "National Evaluation of Weed and Seed." Research in Brief (Office of Justice Programs).

Egley, Arlen, Jr., and James C. Howell. June 2011. *Highlights of the 2009 National Youth Gang Survey*. Juvenile Justice Fact Sheet (U.S. Department of Justice, Office of Justice Programs, Office of Juvenile Justice and Delinquency Prevention).

Evans, Dave. 2006. *Social Networks and Dynamic User Profiles.* ClickZ. Last Modified June 7, 2006. www.clickz.com.

Fassler, David. 2012. "Your Teen's Brain: Driving without the Brakes." *Scientific American* (blog entry). Last Modified March 15, 2012. http://blogs.scientificamerican.com/guest-blog/2012/03/15/your-teens-brain-driving-without-the-brakes/.

Gee, James Paul. 2003. *What Video Games Have to Teach Us About Learning and Literacy.* New York: Palgrave MacMillan.

Grimm, Jr., Robert, John Foster-Bey, David Reingold, and Rebecca Nesbit. December 2006. "Volunteer Growth in America: A Review of Trends Since 1974." Volunteering in America. (Corporation for National and Community Service, Office of Research and Policy Development Authors.)

Gross, Terry. 2012. "Habits: How They Form And How To Break Them." Transcript. NPR, Fresh Air from WHYY. Last Modified March 5, 2012. www.npr.org/templates/transcript/transcript.php?storyId=147192599.

Hammer, Heather, David Finkelhor, Andrea J. Sedlak, and Lorraine E. Porcellini. December 2004. "National Estimates of Missing Children: Selected Trends, 1988–1999." *NISMART.*

Harris Interactive. December 2009. "Scratching the Surface." *Trends and Tudes* 8 (4).

Harris Interactive. February 2008. "Today's Youth: Understanding Their Importance and Influence." *Trends and Tudes* 7 (1).

Harris Interactive. November 2010. "YouthPulse 2010." *Trends and Tudes* 9 (2).

Health Council of East Central Florida, Inc. March 2011. *PKZ Annual Evaluation Report 2009–2010.* City of Orlando. www.cityoforlando.net.

Hoffmann, John P., and Felicia G. Cerbone. May 2002. "Parental Substance Use Disorder and the Risk of Adolescent Drug Abuse: An Event History Analysis." *Drug and Alcohol Dependence* 66 (3): 255–264.

Hockenberry, Sarah, Melissa Sickmund, and Anthony Sladky. July 2011. *Juvenile Residential Facility Census, 2008: Selected Findings.* Juvenile Offenders and Victims: National Report Series (U.S. Department of Justice, Office of Justice Programs, Office of Juvenile Justice and Delinquency Prevention).

Huffman, Fatma G., Sankarabharan Kanikireddy, and Manthan Patel. 2011. "Parenthood—A Contributing Factor to Childhood Obesity." *International Journal of Environmental Research and Public Health*, 7 (7): 2800–2810. doi:10.3390/ijerph7072800.

James, Susan Donaldson. 2008. "Study Reports Anal Sex on Rise Among Teens." *ABC News*. Last Modified December 10, 2008. www.abcnews.go.com/Health.

Johnston, Lloyd D., Patrick M. O'Malley, Jerald G. Bachman, and John E. Schulenberg. 2011. *"Volume 1: Secondary School Students." Monitoring the Future National Survey Results on Drug Use, 1975–2010*. Institute for Social Research, The University of Michigan.

Johnston, Lloyd D., Patrick M. O'Malley, Jerald G. Bachman, and John E. Schulenberg. 2011. *"Volume 1: College Students and Adults Ages 19–50." Monitoring the Future National Survey Results on Drug Use, 1975–2010*. Institute for Social Research, The Unversity of Michigan.

Karageorghis, Costas, and David-Lee Priest. 2012. "Music in Sport and Exercise: An Update on Research and Application." *The Sports Journal*. Accessed March 27, 2012. www.thesportjournal.org/article/music-sport-and-exercise-update-research-and-application.

Lederman, Linda C., and Lea P. Stewart. 2005. *Changing the Culture of College Drinking: A Socially Situated Health Communication Campaign*. Creskill, NJ: Hampton Press.

Lescano, Celia M., Christopher D. Houck, Larry K. Brown, Glenn Doherty, Ralph J. DiClemente, M. Isabel Fernandez, David Pugatch, William E. Schlenger, and Barbara J. Silver. June 2009. "Correlates of Heterosexual Anal Intercourse Among At-Risk Adolescents and Young Adults." *American Journal of Public Health* 99 (6): 1131–1136.

Lillard, Angeline S., and Jennifer Peterson. October 2011. "The Immediate Impact of Different Types of Television on Young Children's Executive Function." *Pediatrics* 128 (4). doi:10.1542/peds.2010-1919

Lippman, Laura. 2009. "Developing Indicators of Youth Contribution." Presented at Youth Contribution Indicators Meeting, Minneapolis, MN, August 13, 2009.

MacDonald, John, Ricky N. Bluthenthal, Daniela Golinelli, Aaron Kofner, Robert J. Stokes, Amber Sehgal, Terry Fain, and Leo Beletsky. 2009. "Neighborhood Effects on Crime and Youth Violence." Technical Report. www.rand.org.

Martinez, Gladys, Casey E. Copen, and Joyce C. Abma. 2011. "Teenagers in the United States: Sexual Activity, Contraceptive Use, and Childbearing, 2006–2010 National Survey of Family Growth." *Vital Health Statistics* 23 (31).

Martin, Suzanne. Winter 2008. *Kids as a Force for Positive Social Change*. Connecticut: The Family Room Strategic Consulting Group, LLC.

Mariano, Willoughby. July 27, 2009. "In Parramore, kids playing replace drug dealers and hookers." *Orlando Sentinel.* www.orlandosentinel.com.

McDonough, Hugh, JoAnn Jastrzab, Cynthia Sipe, and Catherine Rappapport. September 3, 2002. "Mentoring, E-mentoring, and At-risk Youth Literature Review: Final Report." Prepared for The Foundation for Civility.

McGarrell, Edmund F., Natalie Kroovand Hipple, Nicholas Corsaro, Timothy S. Bynum, Heather Perez, Carol A. Zimmermann, and Melissa Garmo. February 2009. *Project Safe Neighborhoods—A National Program to Reduce Gun Crime: Final Project Report.* Final Project Report, Michigan State University.

Michigan Department of Education. March 2002. "What Research Says about Parent Involvement in Children's Education." www.michigan.gov/mde.

Kimberly J. Mitchell, David Finkelhor, Lisa M. Jones and Janis Wolak. January 2012. "Prevalence and Characteristics of Youth Sexting: A National Study." *Pediatrics* 129 (1). doi:10.1542/peds.2011-1730.

Moore, Lynn L., David A. Lombardi, Mary Jo White, James L. Campbell, Susan A. Oliveria, and R. Curtis Ellison. 1991. "Influence of Parents' Physical Activity Levels on Activity Levels of Young Children." *The Journal of Pediatrics* 118 (2): 215–219.

National Center for Missing & Exploited Children. 2012. "Statistics." Accessed March 27, 2012. www.missingkids.com/en_US/documents/Statistics.pdf

The National Center on Addiction and Substance Abuse at Columbia University. September 2011. *The Importance of Family Dinners VII.* New York: The National Center on Addiction and Substance Abuse at Columbia University.

National Institute of Mental Health. 2012. "Suicide in the U.S.: Statistics and Prevention." Accessed January 26, 2012. www.nimh.nih.gov/health/publications/suicide-in-the-us-statistics-and-prevention/index.shtml.

National Sherriff's Association. 2012. "Neighborhood Watch Manual." Accessed March 24, 2012. www.usaonwatch.org/assets/publications/0_NW_Manual_1210.pdf.

National Survey of Children's Health (NSCH). 2003. Data query from the Child and Adolescent Health Measurement Initiative, Data Resource Center for Child and Adolescent Health website. Accessed March 22, 2012. www.childhealthdata.org.

National Survey of Children's Health (NSCH). 2007. Data query from the Child and Adolescent Health Measurement Initiative, Data Resource Center for Child and Adolescent Health website. Accessed March 22, 2012. www.childhealthdata.org.

National Weather Service. 2012. "Medical Aspects of Lightning." Lightning Safety. Accessed March 27, 2012. www.lightningsafety.noaa.gov/medical.htm

The Nemours Foundation/KidsHealth. 2012. "Body Mass Index (BMI) Charts." *Growth & Development*. Accessed March 26, 2012. www.kidshealth.org/parent/growth.

Office of Juvenile Justice and Delinquency Prevention. 2011. "Juveniles in Corrections." Census of Juveniles in Residential Placement 2010, OJJDP Statistical Briefing Book. Last Modified December 9, 2011.

Olsen, Stefanie. 2006. "MySpace Blurs Line Between Friends and Flacks." *CNET News.com*. Last Modified July 31, 2006. www.news.cnet.com.

P/PV. June 2001. "Supporting Mentors: Technical Assistant Packet #6." (Northwest Regional Educational Laboratory).

Puzzanchera, Charles and Benjamin Adams. December 2011. "Juvenile Arrests 2009." Juvenile Offenders and Victims: National Report Series (U.S. Department of Justice, Office of Justice Programs, Office of Juvenile Justice and Delinquency Prevention).

Rhodes, Jean E., and David L. DuBois. 2006. Understanding and Facilitating the Youth Mentoring Movement. Social Policy Report 20, no. 3 (Society for Research in Child Development).

Richtel, Matt. 2012. "Young, in Love and Sharing Everything, Including a Password." *The New York Times*. Last Modified January 17, 2012. www.nytimes.com.

Rideout, Victoria J., Ulla G. Foehr, and Donald F. Roberts. March 2005. "GENERATION M: Media in the Lives of 8- to 18-Year-Olds." A Kaiser Family Foundation Study.

Rideout, Victoria J., Ulla G. Foehr, and Donald F. Roberts. January 2010. "GENERATION M2: Media in the Lives of 8- to 18-Year-Olds." A Kaiser Family Foundation Study.

Scaglioni, Silvia, Michela Salvioni, and Cinzia Galimberti. 2008. "Influence of Parental Attitudes in the Development of Children Eating Behavior." supplement, *British Journal of Nutrition*, 99: S22–S25. doi:10.1017/S0007114508892471.

Sedlak, Andrea J., David Finkelhor, Heather Hammer, and Dana J. Schultz. October 2002. "National Estimates of Missing Children: An Overview."

National Incidence Studies of Missing, Abducted, Runaway, and Thrownaway Children. (U.S. Department of Justice, Office of Justice Programs, Office of Juvenile Justice and Delinquency Prevention.)

Shader, Michael. 2004. Risk Factors for Delinquency: An Overview. (U.S. Department of Justice, Office of Juvenile Justice and Delinquency Prevention.)

Sickmund, Melissa, John T. Sladky, W. Kang, and Charles Puzzanchera. 2012. "Easy Access to the Census of Juveniles in Residential Placement." Accessed January 23, 2012. www.ojjdp.gov/ojstatbb/ezacjrp/.

Skoloff, Brian. 2010. "Warrants Detail Abuse of Kids Buried by Dad." *MSNBC*. Last Modified December 9, 2010. www.msnbc.msn.com/id/40587902/ns/us_news-crime_and_courts/#.T3JSiuwUG8x.

Sprint. 2012. "Parental Controls." Accessed March 29, 2012. http://support.sprint.com/support/service/category/Parental_controls-Parental_controls.

Stahl, Anne L. November 2006. Person Offenses in Juvenile Court, 1985–2002. OJJDP Fact Sheet, no. 3.(U.S. Department of Justice, Office of Justice Programs, Office of Juvenile Justice and Delinquency Prevention.)

Substance Abuse and Mental Health Services Administration. 2011. Results from the 2010 National Survey on Drug Use and Health: Summary of National Findings. Center for Behavioral Health Statistics and Quality. www.oas.samhsa.gov/NSDUH/2k10NSDUH/2k10Results.htm#6.3.

Suicide.org. 2012. "Suicide Statistics." Accessed March 20, 2012. www.suicide.org/suicide-statistics.html#death-rates

Tierney, Joseph, Jean Baldwin Grossman, and Nancy Resch. September 2000. *Making a Difference: An Impact Study of Big Brothers Big Sisters.* Public/Private Ventures. www.ppv.org.

T-Mobile. 2012. "Safety." Accessed March 28, 2012. http://family.t-mobile.com/safety-and-security#helping-kids-use-cells-responsibly.

Topor, David R., Susan P. Keane, Terri L. Shelton, and Susan D. Calkins. 2010. "Parent Involvement and Student Academic Performance: A Multiple Mediational Analysis." *Journal of Prevention & Intervention in the Community* 38 (3): 183–197. doi:10.1080/10852352.2010.486297.

University Outreach & Engagement. June 2004. "Parent Involvement in Schools." Best Practice Briefs (Michigan State University) no. 30.

United States Congress, Senate Committee of the Judiciary, Subcommittee to Investigate Juvenile Delinquency. 1955b. *Juvenile Delinquency (Television Programs), Hearings, 84th Congress, 1st Session*, April 6–7. Washington, DC: United States Government Printing Office.

U.S. Census Bureau. 2011. *Statistical Abstract of the United States.* 131st ed. Washington. www.census.gov/compendia/statab/.

U.S. Department of Justice. 2012. "Forcible Rape." Uniform Crime Report, Crime in the United States, 2010. Accessed March 30, 2012. www.fbi.gov/about-us/cjis/ucr/crime-in-the-u.s/2010/crime-in-the-u.s.-2010/violent-crime/rapemain.

Verizon Wireless. 2012. "Verizon Safeguards." Accessed March 29, 2012. https://wbillpay.verizonwireless.com/vzw/nos/uc/uc_verizon_safeguards_logout.jsp.

VGChartz. 2012 "Game Database." Accessed March 29, 2012. www.vgchartz.com/gamedb.

Wilson, Jeremy M., Steven Chermak, and Edmund F. McGarrell. 2010. "Community-Based Violence Prevention: An Assessment of Pittsburgh's One Vision One Life Program." Technical Report. www.rand.org.

Ybarra, Michele L., and Kimberly J. Mitchell. February 1, 2008. "How Risky Are Social Networking Sites? A Comparison of Places Online Where Youth Sexual Solicitation and Harassment Occurs." *Pediatrics,* 121 (2): e350–e357. doi:10.1542/peds.2007-0693.

Index